The Children of Nazis

The Sons and Daughters of Himmler, Göring,
Höss, Mengele, and Others—
Living with a Father's Monstrous Legacy

Tania Crasnianski

Translated by Molly Grogan

Arcade Publishing • New York

Copyright © Editions Grasset & Fasquelle, 2016
English-language translation copyright © 2018 by Skyhorse Publishing, Inc.

All rights reserved. No part of this book may be reproduced in any manner
without the express written consent of the publisher, except in the case of brief
excerpts in critical reviews or articles. All inquiries should be addressed to Arcade
Publishing, 307 West 36th Street, 11th Floor, New York, NY 10018.

First English-language edition

First published in France in 2016 under the title *Enfants de Nazis*

Arcade Publishing books may be purchased in bulk at special discounts for
sales promotion, corporate gifts, fund-raising, or educational purposes. Special
editions can also be created to specifications. For details, contact the Special Sales
Department, Arcade Publishing, 307 West 36th Street, 11th Floor, New York, NY
10018 or arcade@skyhorsepublishing.com.

Arcade Publishing® is a registered trademark of Skyhorse Publishing, Inc.®,
a Delaware corporation.

Visit our website at www.arcadepub.com.

10 9 8 7 6 5 4 3 2 1

Crasnianski, Tania, author.
Title: The children of Nazis : the sons and daughter of Himmler, Göring,
Höss, Mengele, and others : living with a father's monstrous legacy / by
Tania Crasnianski ; translated from the French by Molly Grogan.
Other titles: Enfants de Nazis. French | Sons and daughter of Himmler,
Göring, Höss, Mengele, and others | Living with a father's monstrous
legacy
Description: New York : Arcade Publishing, [2016]
Identifiers: LCCN 2017035834 (print) | LCCN 2017036773 (ebook) | ISBN
9781628728088 (ebook) | ISBN 9781628728057 (hardcover : alk. paper)
Subjects: LCSH: Children of Nazis--Biography. | Nazis--Family relationships.
| Nazis--Germany--Biography.
Classification: LCC DD243 (ebook) | LCC DD243 .C37 2016 (print) | DDC
943.086092/2--dc23

Cover design by Brian Peterson

Printed in the United States of America

For the children

For Satya, Aliocha, Ilya, and Arthur

CONTENTS

PREFACE

This book presents the portraits of eight children and is the result of extensive research into the different existing archives, legal documents, letters, books, articles, and interviews touching on the personal lives of Nazi leaders and their descendants. None of these portraits is anonymous. Other books have preserved the anonymity of these individuals; I have chosen to name them, so that the weight of these legacies might be fully appreciated. It is also true that some of these sons and daughters feel it is easier to be the "child of" certain of these men rather than others.

My initial intention was to meet every one of my subjects. In the end, I interviewed only one: Niklas Frank. Some of these descendants are no longer alive; others would have had nothing to add to the content of earlier interviews. Then there are those who are no longer willing to revisit the past and still others, such as Gudrun Himmler and Edda Göring, who have almost always refused to speak of their fathers.

So that the reader might get an immediate sense of what these lives were like, each portrait opens with a significant episode, freely imagined.

REGARDING TRANSLATIONS

In the original French edition, translations from German were made into French by the author, and corrected by the translator Olivier Mannoni. In this edition, all content is translated from French, except in the case of English-language sources, which have been quoted in the original.

INTRODUCTION

Gudrun, Edda, Martin, Niklas, and the rest . . .

These children have a secret. They are the sons and daughters of Göring, Hess, Frank, Bormann, Höss, Speer, and Mengele: the criminals who orchestrated the darkest period of contemporary history.

Yet their story is not recorded in the history books.

Their fathers committed the greatest evil possible and then surrendered their humanity without the slightest hesitation when they pleaded "not guilty" to the charges brought against them at Nuremberg. Will history remember that these men were fathers as well? After the war, a collective movement was aimed at placing responsibility for Nazi Germany's crimes and extermination policies solely on the Third Reich's principal leaders and absolving lesser dignitaries and Nazis, who hid behind a convenient formula: "All that was Hitler."

Who are these individuals whose lives are discussed in this

book? They share a common heritage: the extermination of millions of innocent people by their fathers. Their names will forever live in infamy.

Must anyone feel responsible, or even guilty, for the crimes of his parents? Family life leaves an indelible mark on every child. An inheritance as sinister as theirs cannot come without consequences. "Like father, like son," we say. "A father has two lives: his and his son's." What became of the offspring of Nazi leaders? How did they live with such macabre facts?

When one unrepentant Nazi was questioned along these lines by his granddaughter, an Israeli Jew, he gave her this answer: "The guilty one is the one who feels guilty!" Without batting an eye, he also made this suggestion: "Put all that behind you. Life is much simpler afterwards."[1]

It is very difficult for children to judge their parents. We lack distance and objectivity when we look at the people who brought us into the world and raised us. The stronger the emotional ties, the more complicated such a judgment becomes. When a family's history is so disturbing, what choices does it have while living with its knowledge? Embracing it? Rejecting it outright? The responses of these children are diametrically opposed at times. Some have adopted their fathers' positions. Few are neutral. Some have strongly denounced their fathers' actions, yet continue to feel love and affection for them. Still others refuse to love a "monster," so they deny their fathers' involvement, in order to preserve the unconditional love of a child for a parent. Finally, there are those who have moved into hatred and total rejection. They carry this past from day to day like a ball and chain; it is impossible to ignore. Some have denied nothing, some have turned to religion, some have even had themselves sterilized so they can never "transmit the evil" to their children, and some believed they could eliminate their "bad" genes by masturbating! Whether they have chosen to deny, suppress, or support their fathers, or feel guilty themselves, all of them have taken a position—consciously or unconsciously—on the past.

Most of these children live or lived in Germany. Some converted to Catholicism or Judaism, and some were even ordained as priests or rabbis. Is this a strategy to keep quiet their fate of having been born to a criminal? Aharon Shear-Yashuv became a rabbi in the Israel Defense Forces, even though his father was neither a Nazi official nor one of its principal underlings. While a theology student, Aharon, born Wolfgang Schmidt, decided against becoming a Catholic priest, since he was never a believer. His conversion to Judaism, he insists, is not directly tied to the Holocaust: "Though there is a particularism in Judaism on the one hand, on the other there is a lot of openness. It is a fact that converts are accepted—not only that—but a convert can even become a rabbi and serve as a major and chaplain in the Israeli Defense Force!"[2]

Dan Bar-On, a professor of psychology at Ben-Gurion University, interprets this type of conversion as a strategy: "If you become part of the victim community, you get rid of the burden of being part of the perpetrator community."[3] Is this an attempt to escape, rather than face, the past? The children who converted offer divergent responses, yet a spiritual calling has allowed some of them to put the past behind them.

In postwar Germany's self-imposed silence as the country began to rebuild, the Nazis' descendants had to struggle to put themselves back together.

My own grandfather was a career air force man who retired to a secluded hunting lodge in the Black Forest. Although I was very close to him, he never spoke about his time in the armed forces. He is not unusual; the war's shadow hung over Germany and France for many long years, and still does, although tongues have loosened. When I was a child, we accepted this diktat of silence. Like my grandfather, the postwar generations avoided the subject. Some people finally adhered to the reigning mutism and never spoke of the war again, for fear of tarnishing the image they held of their parents. Would they have really wanted to know who their parents were during the war and the role they played in Germany's most sinister period? Nothing is less certain. The transmission of knowledge never took place. To flee the past, my German mother chose, at the age of twenty, to live by herself in France. She always wanted to be French and could not understand my decision to write this book. Why this subject? Why keep talking about it? These are questions we don't often ask.

I am German, French, and Russian, but of the three, my German side has shaped my personality the most. I could not escape Germany's history. Anne Weber frames the problem this way: "Is this a burden we inherit at birth? It is there at the beginning and it never goes away. No Russian is the representation of the Gulag, no French person is the embodiment of the French Revolution or colonialism; they each have their national history."[4] Germany, however, is always identified with Nazism.

My interest in society's marginalized led me to study prisons and then to become a criminal lawyer. I hope that this profession has taught me the necessary rigor to evoke historical facts and the perceptions held by the Nazi children featured in this book. It is my wish, through these examples, to understand the implications of the past for a world whose future we try desperately to direct.

Truth and reality can be heavy burdens to carry. There are those who prefer to keep their family secrets locked up, even if they have never learned precisely what they are. Not one of these Nazi officials had the courage or the strength to explain to his children the crimes he committed.

Most of these Nazi children chose not to change their names, perhaps because they are haunted by them. Some, as in the case of the sons of Albert Speer and Martin Bormann, even carry the same first name as their father. Matthias Göring, the great-nephew of Hermann Göring, has said he likes his name; others insist that a name is of no importance. As for Eichmann's son, he does not see the point: "Change my name? What would have been the point? You cannot escape from yourself, from the past."[5] Still others, such as Gudrun Himmler and Edda Göring, are proud of their family names and venerate their fathers.

"Even when I was carrying out exterminations, I led a normal family life," declared Rudolf Höss, the Kommandant of Auschwitz.[6] How is such a contradiction possible? In dissociative identity disorders, two contradictory impulses exist in a single personality, which may provide one explanation for how Hitler's lieutenants could exterminate millions of people, all the while living a normal life at home. How could these monsters kiss their children goodbye before going to coldly kill or order the killing of men, women, and children? Is it even possible to imagine Himmler kissing his *Püppi*, his little doll, on his way to headquarters to sign an execution order for children, just because they were Jews?

It would be convenient and reassuring if these criminals could be labeled with specific pathologies that would explain their atrocities. Those who have looked closely into the question, however, have never demonstrated a common personality type in these men. During Eichmann's trial in Jerusalem, one of his examining psychiatrists found his behavior toward his wife and children, parents, siblings, and friends "not only normal but most desirable."[7] It is tempting to believe that such people are bloodthirsty monsters; in fact, their "normalcy" is even more terrifying. "Monsters exist, but they are too few in number to be truly dangerous; more dangerous are the common men," observed Primo Levi.[8]

In her controversial work, *Eichmann in Jerusalem*, Hannah Arendt identified the "banality of evil," a concept she illustrated using the example of a dolefully ordinary but zealous civil servant who never thought about what he was doing and who proved incapable of distinguishing right from wrong. Arendt does not exonerate him but she does insist how inhumanity can lodge deep within each of us and that it is imperative to continue to think, to never stop listening to reason, to always question oneself, so as to never sink into the same banality of evil.

The children who are the subject of this book only knew one aspect of their fathers' personalities. The other would be reported to them after Germany's surrender. They were too young during the war to understand or even perceive what was happening. Born between 1922 and 1944, the oldest were not even eighteen years old during the height of the war. Their childhood memories are often limited to the green pastures of Bavaria. Many lived in the secure perimeter around the Berghof, the Führer's mountain chalet at Obersalzberg in the Bavarian Alps, south of Munich near the Austrian border. This isolated spot, reserved for the Führer's use, was untouched by the war and its violence. After the war, and for many years, the Third Reich was not even mentioned in the curriculum taught in German schools.

Are their parents monsters? "If with the best will in the world one cannot extract any diabolical or demonic profundity from Eichmann, that is still far from calling it commonplace," Hannah Arendt wrote in *Eichmann in Jerusalem*.[9] The prosecution attempted to portray him as "the most abnormal monster the world had ever seen";[10] however, Arendt's view was that he was a "mere functionary" who was "terrifyingly normal."[11] "More normal, at any rate, than I am after having examined him,"[12] one psychiatrist who examined Eichmann during his 1961 trial exclaimed. According to Arendt, "Nothing would have been farther from his mind than to determine with Richard III 'to prove a villain.'"[13] Eichmann described himself as a gentle man who couldn't bear the sight of blood. "His was . . . no case of insane hatred of Jews, of fanatical anti-Semitism or indoctrination of any kind," Arendt concluded.[14] What allowed him to become one of the greatest criminals of his time was his "sheer thoughtlessness—something by no means identical with stupidity."[15] This shortcoming manifested itself as well in his "almost total inability ever to look at anything from the other fellow's point of view"[16] and in his lapses of memory. "What he had done he had done, he did not want to deny it . . . By this he did not mean to say that he regretted anything," Arendt reported, since he believed that "repentance is for little children."[17] For Arendt, mere thoughtlessness can suffice to create one of history's greatest criminals. Eichmann was no less guilty for his lack of a moral conscience.

Nevertheless, all of these Nazis thought of themselves as

moral beings. Heinrich Himmler, the architect of the Final Solution, was convinced he was one.[18] Harald Welzer observed that during the Third Reich, killing became a socially acceptable act. The morality of murder that was particular to National Socialism enabled its executors to remain within the bounds of propriety while killing. As absurd as that seems today, the Reich's normative framework permitted killing on the argument that it was necessary to ensure Germany's survival, based on the irreducible inequality of human beings.[19]

The human beings with whom I am concerned here judge their fathers in a normative moral framework that has shifted since the time period in which they lived. Some legitimize or justify their fathers' actions by arguing that under the standard framework that was theirs, these actions were legitimate. A son of Joachim von Ribbentrop, who was Hitler's foreign minister, has said, "My father only did what he thought was right. Under the same circumstances, I would make the same decisions he did. He was only one of Hitler's advisors but, in reality, Hitler did not take anyone's advice. My father's sole desire was to do his duty as a German. He foresaw the immense danger that was arriving from the East. History proved him right."[20] Like him, Gudrun Himmler delivered a "not guilty" verdict on her father, Heinrich Himmler, and she would stand by that opinion her entire life. Himmler would have made the same case for himself at the Nuremberg trials, even if he had not committed suicide before they opened.

Gustave M. Gilbert, an American psychologist who studied the principal Nazi criminals whose fates were decided at Nuremberg, concluded that the distinguishing feature of these men was their lack of empathy for others, and he showed that executioners are less likely to experience depression than their victims because they are convinced they are good men who have no choice but to follow orders.

This is not exactly the case of their children who learned about their fathers' actions after the war, when the Nazis' heresies had been exposed and the legitimacy of the solution to the "Jewish problem" had been vigorously condemned.

Often, they examine the past through the lens of their own childhoods. Some only remember how much they were loved; this is often the case of single children, frequently sons, but above all daughters: Gudrun Himmler (Himmler's only legitimate daughter); Edda Göring, the daughter of the Reichsmarschall; or Irene Rosenberg, the daughter of the chief Nazi Party ideologist and the Reich Minister for the Occupied Eastern Territories, Alfred Rosenberg. All three were cosseted children who worshipped their fathers and remained sympathetic to Nazism. Many other descendants, demonstrating a curious belief that their common history is quantifiable, think their personal stories are easier to bear than those of other children of Nazi dignitaries.

In order to better grasp their stories, each chapter includes a reminder of the father's position in the National Socialist hierarchy, the ways in which the child was steeped in the ideals of the historical period, and the mother's role in the child's education. Identifying, as closely as possible, the dynamics of the early home environment is crucial to understanding their stories.

The descendants of certain key figures of the Third Reich are missing from this book. For example, all six children of Joseph Goebbels, the Reich Minister of Propaganda, were killed by their parents in the Führer's bunker. Goebbels's wife, Magda, had a son from her first marriage to Günther Quant, who in turn had a daughter who converted to Judaism at the age of twenty-four. Quant, a businessman and a German Jew, was sent to the concentration camps.

Hitler himself had no children by choice: "Think of the problems if I had children! In the end they would try to make my son my successor. Besides, the chances are slim for someone like me to have a capable son. That is almost always how it goes in such cases. Consider Goethe's son—a completely worthless person!"[21]

More than seventy years later, it is still difficult to write about this subject. Through all the stages of this book, I refrained from judging these children. They cannot be held responsible for actions they did not commit, even if some of them deny none of their fathers' actions. Is that a form of self-defense, in the face of an indefensible past?

Gudrun Himmler is the perfect illustration.

GUDRUN HIMMLER

Nazism's "Poppet"

Every year since 1958, a tiny mountain village in the Austrian section of the Bohemian Forest hosts Third Reich nostalgia seekers from all over Europe. In the bucolic setting of an ancient Celtic holy site, these middle-age men in glad rags gather every autumn to greet their former comrades. Young neo-Nazis also attend, to mingle with the veterans. Among this group of former Nazis and personalities aligned to the far-right, everyone agrees that the Waffen-SS simply fulfilled their duty. The attendees praise the soldiers' sense of sacrifice and sometimes even go so far as to argue that they were victims.

Behind the drawn curtains of a local guesthouse, a man chants slogans to the glory of the great Germany. He takes pleasure in galvanizing his listeners as his own mentor did before him. His goal is to re-create the ambiance and the enthusiasm that Hitler aroused when he gave speeches in Munich's brasseries. Decades have passed, but the ideals of the group that has gathered are the same as they ever were. Some of the men proudly wear their German military medals from World War II, the Iron Cross, or the Knight's Cross of the Iron Cross, always with a swastika in the center. They speak in excited tones about the time of the German people's superiority, of the national community that required complete self-sacrifice, unfailing loyalty, and the rejection of any humanitarian sentiments for the "inner enemies" of the nation.[1] This society of conspirators still believes in the quest for greatness and the motto of the SS: "Our honor is loyalty."

A special guest sits at a distance from the others, where she can receive smaller groups of guests within the circle of her admirers. Only a privileged few are invited in. Her face is hard, weathered by time and bitterness, but she has lost nothing of her verve. Her fine white hair is gathered into a small chignon at the base of her skull, and she wears proudly on her blouse a silver brooch: four horse heads arranged in a circle to form a swastika.

From behind her glasses, two small, ice-blue eyes grip her terrified interlocutors. They idolize her, this singular heiress of the great Germany, the "Nazi princess," Gudrun Himmler.

The "princess" enjoys watching the faithful parade before her, asking them in turn in an inquisitorial voice: "Where were you during the war? What was your unit?" From her father, whom she sometimes accompanied on his inspection rounds, she learned military logistics and keen powers of observation. This time, it is the war veterans' parade, and they are proud to show themselves to the daughter of Hitler's right-hand man. As they recite name and rank for her, they almost feel transported back to the time when their authority reigned supreme in the world. For a moment, some small bit of their lost pride returns to these men who must hide their past on a daily basis.

"Fifth SS Panzer Division Wiking,"[2] announces an intimidated-looking man who has just entered the room. She questions him: "Were you a volunteer in the Danish Waffen-SS?"

"Absolutely," is the answer from this sixty-eight-year-old veteran. His name is Vagner Kristensen, born in 1927 on the Danish island of Fyn. What explains the deference and fear that he shows to this tiny woman? Is it that, having lived in her father's shadow for so many years, whether he was present or not, she has adopted his gestures, his voice? Her goal in life: exonerate her father's reputation, to merit being her father's daughter. Heinrich Himmler had eyes only for her, his one and only legitimate child, and she returns the favor.

On this day, Gudrun Himmler also meets Sören Kam, SS-Nr 456059, a Danish Nazi implicated in 1943 in the murder of an anti-Nazi journalist but never convicted. He fled to Germany and has lived trouble-free in Bavaria ever since. His name is on the list of most wanted Nazi criminals, yet he is a free man. Her father would be so proud of her due to her confidence before these men, in contrast to himself, who had to battle an inferiority complex and difficulties with interpersonal relationships.

As a young girl, she was so afraid of disappointing him that she swore her mother to secrecy whenever she made a mistake or behaved badly. She is convinced of his innocence; she is sure he never committed any of the crimes of which he was accused and she considers his guilty verdict completely unwarranted. She hoped for a long time to write a book that would exonerate him, rather than defend him, which would imply guilt.

Gudrun is certain that, one day, his name will be remembered "in the same breath as Napoleon, Wellington, or Moltke."[3]

History, however, will forever condemn him.

On Wednesday afternoons, her father sometimes brought her along on inspections, usually at Dachau, the first of the Nazi concentration camps in Germany. The camp was Himmler's idea, and it opened in March 1933, a few kilometers from Munich. "The ones with a red triangle are prisoners. A black triangle is for criminals," he explained to her. The little girl thought they all looked like prisoners, unshaven and poorly clothed. She was more interested in the vegetable garden and the greenhouse. "My father explained to me the properties of the different herbs and he let me pick some of the leaves," she would later remember.[4] She was twelve years old when she made this grim visit; the plants reminded her of her childhood on a farm where she liked to help her mother tend the garden. A photo was taken that day at Dachau. In it, a little blonde girl in a black coat smiles for the camera. She looks happy, surrounded by her father, Reinhard Heydrich, the future director of the Gestapo, and Karl Wolff, Himmler's aide-de-camp. They pose under a sign showing prisoners where to line up.

Gudrun watched with admiration as her father rose through the ranks. In August 1943, she wrote in her diary: "Pappi Reichsinnenminister, that makes me incredibly happy."[5] In July 1942, as he was traveling to Auschwitz to review preparations for the Final Solution, which required the large-scale use of the gas Zyklon B, he coolly closed a letter to his wife, as if he were oblivious to what he was doing: "I leave for Auschwitz. I kiss you, Your Heini."[6] In his letters, he provides no indications as to his movements or activities and says not a word about the extermination of the Jewish people. He reveals only that he has much work and important assignments to complete. The same man will calmly justify his atrocities. "Concerning the Jewish women and children, I did not consider that I had the right to allow these children to grow up to become avengers who would kill our sons and grandsons in turn. That would have been cowardly on my part. As a result, the question was resolved without any need of discussion."[7]

Though Gudrun was the daughter of the Reichsführer of the Schutzstaffel (SS), the fanatical and uncontested master of the Third Reich's most dreaded agency, her story is not told in the history books. Heinrich Himmler's childhood friends remembered that he was incapable of killing a fly.[8] As an adult, he became the chief of the Gestapo and the SS and the architect of the concentration camps and of the extermination of Europe's Jews.

Heinrich Himmler met Gudrun's mother, Margarete Siegroth (née Boden), a divorced nurse, in 1927, in a train traveling from Munich to Berchtesgaden, near the Austrian border. He was twenty-seven years old, on the puny side, nearsighted, with a receding chin. Looking nothing like the ideal Aryan, he had an inferiority complex about his appearance. His weak physique and fragile stomach ruled out sports and drunken fraternizing. A soldier who never saw active service, he developed an obsession with discipline and uniforms, which helped him shore up his confidence. As a young man, he remained so inexperienced with women that he took the tack of extolling the advantages of sexual abstinence.[9] Later, he would regret not having sown his wild oats in his youth; he had his first sexual experience at the age of twenty-eight. Margarete, or "Marga" for short, was tall and blonde with blue eyes, and a Protestant: an ideal Aryan woman. Himmler's seduction strategy was to supply her with books about Freemasonry and the "global Jewish conspiracy." The German economy was listing, and the country was in need of both a "savior" and scapegoats. Marga was not immune to the ambient anti-Semitism. "Once a Jew always a Jew,"[10] she would conclude about her partner in the clinic she owned when she sold her shares in it, following her introduction to Himmler.

Shy Heinrich wrote her romantic letters, sometimes signing off with "Your landsknecht," referencing a heroic, solitary, and brutal mercenary soldier of the sixteenth and seventeenth centuries. "We must be happy," she responded to him, but their marriage was a union more of affection than love. Marga was seven years Heinrich's senior and would never be accepted by his Catholic family, least of all by his very pious mother. Marga was a divorced Protestant Prussian, anxious and ill at ease in society. The Himmlers worried she would stain their good reputation, and they did not attend Heinrich and Marga's wedding on July 3, 1928, in Berlin-Schöneberg. Gudrun was born August 8, 1929, a blue-eyed girl weighing eight pounds and measuring twenty-one inches. She would become Heinrich Himmler's only legitimate daughter, his *püppi*, his little doll.

Was Gudrun named after Heinrich's favorite childhood book, *The Saga of Gudrun*? It sings the praises of the virtuous Norsewoman, for whom any man would lay down his life. Marga proved unable to bear more children, and the couple later adopted the son of a deceased SS soldier. However, the boy would never feel the warmth of a loving family in their home. In her diary, Marga noted the boy's "criminal nature,"[11] calling him a liar and even a thief. They sent him eventually to a boarding school and finally to a section of the National Political Academy, which functioned as a high school for the future

Nazi elite. Gudrun, on the other hand, was the very image of perfection; Marga never tired of recording in her journal how pleasant and sweet she was: "*Püppi ist liebe u. nett.*" Elsewhere, writing about the Germanization of Poland, she noted, "I read this to Püppi and explained what it means: trek and homecoming to the Fatherland. It is an incredible achievement. People will still be talking about this after thousands of years."[12]

Having studied agronomy at the University of Munich, Heinrich invested his wife's dowry in a chicken farm in neighboring Waldtrudering in 1928. The newlyweds dreamed of being farmers, and Heinrich intended to live there with his wife and daughter. For the most part, however, Marga and Gudrun rarely saw Heinrich, and Marga managed the farm by herself. Moreover, the hens laid few eggs, the chicks died, and the whole scheme was soon going south. Marga complained of Heinrich's frequent absences—which eventually extended into a permanent one—and she sank into depression. The more Heinrich was absent, the more irascible, aggressive, and scornful Margarete became. The Himmlers sold the farm and moved to the center of Munich in 1933. The "nice little man" with a good, though likely inconstant heart," [13] in the eyes of party leaders, became, in reality, Commander of Political Police and then Chief of German Police for the Interior Ministry, heading up the SS in June 1936. Reichsführer-SS Himmler was a cold and calculating Great Inquisitor who could finally get the upper hand on his inferiority complexes by developing an obsession for racial purity.

After a short stay in Munich between 1936 and 1937, the Himmlers moved to Lake Tegernsee in Upper Bavaria, where Heinrich had purchased a house in the township of Gmund in 1934. However, as he took on ever-greater responsibility within the party, Himmler abandoned his wife and became sexually active, developing an interest for different aspects of sexuality in society. He acquiesced that Marga was not to blame for her sterility but he was not ready to resign himself to the prospect of fathering no further children. He considered monogamy "the work of Satan,"[14] and an invention of the Catholic Church that deserved to be abolished. He based his ideas on Germanic prehistory: a free, racially pure Norseman could enter into a second marriage provided children were born of it.[15] Himmler allowed his officers experiencing problems in their marriages to divorce or to take a mistress. In his opinion, a healthy man should not content himself for life with one woman and he believed that bigamy would force women to compete for the favors of men.

For certain SS leaders, bigamy and polygamy were also useful tools to keep birthrates up during wartime. Reich Minister of Propaganda Joseph Goebbels, for example, before marrying the woman who would bear him six children, had her make a prenuptial agreement with him, allowing him to have extra-marital relations. Similarly, the wife of Martin Bormann, head of the Nazi Party Chancellery and a close advisor to Hitler, had ten children before dreaming up a scheme to support "the cause" by housing her husband's mistresses under her own roof. Her goal: "[P]ut all the children together in the house on the lake, and live together."[16] The Bormanns believed strongly that a law should be passed allowing "healthy, productive men to have two wives . . . So many worthy women are destined to remain childless. . . . We need children from these women as well!"[17] Bormann wanted to ban the term "illegitimate" and forbid use of the expression "have an affair" because of its pejorative connotation.

To remedy the low birthrate during wartime, Himmler proposed legalizing births out of wedlock in the hope of encouraging more of them. This led to the creation, in 1936, of *Aktion Lebensborn*: a breeding program that encouraged anonymous births by unmarried Aryan mothers. Moreover, aiming to discourage homosexuality, Himmler promoted occasions for adolescents of the opposite sex to meet. In the speech he delivered about homosexuality in Bad Tölz on February 18, 1937, he declared: "I consider it necessary to ensure that young boys between the ages of fifteen and sixteen years meet girls at a dance class, a social evening, or at any variety of occasions. It is at the age of fifteen or sixteen (experience has proven) that young boys go through a period of instability. If he finds a girl to dance with or has a young love, he will be saved, he will retreat from danger."[18] This is hardly the Himmler who, as a young man, sang the praises of abstinence.

In 1940, Himmler separated from Marga rather than divorce her, out of respect for the mother of his child. He was careful afterward to remain close to his daughter whom he adored and cherished more than anything. Despite his growing role in the Nazi Party and his frequent absences, he wished to remain a good father and a proper husband. Posing in childhood photos next to her Travel-Papa, as she liked to call him, Püppi is the image of a little angel in traditional Bavarian dress with a sweet expression and blonde braids that were sometimes rolled into buns over each ear: the perfect German child. Her father gave her regular reports about his daily activities, frequently sent her photos of himself, and generally spent as much time with her as he could. The pocket calendars he kept reveal almost daily phone calls to his wife and daughter. Himmler recorded everything to the last detail, such as, "played with the children" or "conversation with Püppi."[19]

Her poor grades infuriated him. In his opinion, obedience, neatness, and schooling were central to a child's education. Himmler himself displayed unfailing obedience as a child and was always a good student. For her part, Marga kept a record of her daughter's childhood from her earliest years, noting her good behavior, her early predilection for tidiness, or, on the contrary, the trouble Marga had trying to make Gudrun obey her. When Heinrich would visit, he would take her hunting and for walks in the forest. She liked to pick flowers and collect mosses.

The Führer was a central figure in Gudrun's childhood. One night in 1935, two years after Hitler became chancellor, little Gudrun was having trouble falling asleep. "Must Uncle Hitler also die?" she asked her mother anxiously. Marga reassured her that he would certainly live to his hundredth birthday at least, to which the little girl answered with relief, "No, Mother, I know he will live to see two hundred."[20]

The Himmlers were flattered and pleased by the attention the Führer paid to their daughter. In her diary, dated May 3, 1938, Marga wrote: "The Führer visited. Poppet was very excited. It was wonderful to have him to ourselves over supper."[21]

At every New Year, the Führer gave Gudrun a doll and a box of chocolates.

Beginning in late 1938, Himmler began a relationship with one of his secretaries, Hedwig Potthast, who had been working for him for two years. He decided to inform Marga, in the event that he might become a father again. In conformity with his policy of encouraging out-of-wedlock births—a position he would defend publicly in 1940—two children were born: a boy, Helge (1942), followed by a girl, Nanette Dorothea (1944). Helge is Germanic for "healthy, racially pure, and therefore happy," but the boy was nothing like the noble heir Himmler had hoped for.[22] Instead, he was troubled by a dermatological condition, a weak constitution, and excessive shyness.

In 1942, Himmler moved his second family into roomy lodgings, the *Schneewinkellehen* house in Schönau, near Hitler's retreat in Berchtesgaden. Hedwig Potthast and her two children would remain there until the Allied occupation. Hedwig agreed to the arrangement in the hope of being reunited with Himmler after the war. The Allies described her as "a stereotypical Nazi woman."[23] She was Marga's opposite: cheerful, friendly, and on good terms with Himmler's entourage. When Marga learned of the affair, she remarked wearily in her diary: "That only occurs to men once they are rich and highly regarded. Otherwise, older women have to help to feed them or put up with them."[24] In her letters to her husband, however, she never mentioned his mistress or his second family.

Gudrun was often alone, or, when her parents were away, in the care of her mother's sister, Lydia Boden. Beginning in 1939, Marga, wishing to contribute to the war effort, returned to nursing, mostly for the Red Cross in Berlin. She traveled at times to the occupied territories; in Poland in 1940, she allowed herself to comment: "Such a pack of Jews, these Polaks; most of them don't look anything at all like human beings, and such indescribable filth. Cleaning it up is an endless task." Or, "These Polish people don't die very quickly of contagious diseases, they have immunity [sic]! Hard to believe."[25]

Gudrun never went far from Gmund. Under questioning at

Nuremberg on September 22, 1945, she explained that "during the war, we never went anywhere. For five years, we lived in that house and I went to school; that is all that I did."[26] Himmler had refused to bring Marga and Gudrun to Berlin due to the intensifying air raids. Püppi waited every day for her parents to return, but mostly for the brief and sporadic visits of her father. She suffered from stomachaches and was an anxious girl, whose grades at school declined steadily over time.[27] However, she followed the news of the war with great interest. She feared for her father.

Marga remarked in her journal that Gudrun heard many things that a girl should never know.[28] Her father, on the other hand, wanted Marga to explain as much as possible to Gudrun, no matter that she was too young to understand most of it.[29] On June 22, 1941, Hitler launched the invasion of the Soviet Union, opening up the Eastern front, with Operation Barbarossa. It was a Sunday, and Gudrun, who was twelve, wrote to her father: "It's terrible that we are going to war with Russia. They were our allies after all. Russia is so big; the struggle will be very difficult if we want to conquer all of Russia."[30]

Gudrun seems to be aware of the Nazi fantasy, one shared by the Reich's leaders, of a greater Germany reaching as far as the Ural Mountains. Her diary entry dated November 1, 1943: "My parents bought another large garden plot. Up behind the greenhouse as far as the back of the woods, next to the large meadow. The prisoners have moved the fence from inside our current garden. When peace comes we are sure to get an estate in the East. The estate would then bring us more money and make it possible to renovate the house in Gmund. So that the hallways are lighter and we get bigger rooms. Later Haus Lindenfycht will belong to me. When peace comes again we are going to move into the Reich Ministry of the Interior. Maybe we will even get a house at Obersalzberg. Yes, once we have peace again, but that will take a long, long time (2, 3 years)."[31]

In July 1944, she realized Germany was losing the war, yet, as news arrived of the Allied invasion of Normandy and the Soviet offensive on the Eastern Front, she banished the thought of defeat from her mind: "We all believe so firmly in victory (Pappi) that I, as the daughter of the man who is now especially respected and beloved, have to think so too—and I do. It would be unthinkable if we were to lose."[32] Also in July, Himmler ordered the construction of an air-raid shelter on the grounds of the house in Gmund by a work detail of prisoners from Dachau.

Gudrun had few playmates. Her mother was not on good relations with either her husband's family or her own, with the exception of her sister. Isolated from other human contact, Gudrun suffered the caprices of her increasingly irritable mother. When the family of Gebhrard Himmler, Heinrich's oldest brother, came to live with them in the house in Gmund, the conflict between her mother and her aunt soured her relations with her first cousins. Over the course of the war and the defeat, and until his death in 1945, Gudrun saw her father no more than fifteen to twenty times.[33] When he did visit, he stayed only three or four days at the most. She contented herself with telephone calls and the letters he sent her regularly, which included autographed photographs of himself. He also sent clothing and food: chocolates, cheese, and sweets. One day, she received one hundred and fifty tulips from Holland. At the end of the war, when staples were exceedingly rare and hard to come by, Himmler managed to send food packages to the family. On March 5, 1945, Gudrun wrote in her diary: "We no longer have any allies in Europe, and can only rely on ourselves. And among our own people there is *so much* betrayal. . . . The general mood is at zero. . . . The Luftwaffe is still so bad. Göring does not seem to care about anything, that windbag. Goebbels is doing a lot, but he always shows off. They all get medals and awards, except Pappi, and he should be the first to get one. . . . The people all look up to him. He always stays in the background and never shows off."[34]

Gudrun saw her father for the last time at Gmund in November 1944. He stayed for two days. She spoke to him on the phone for the last time in March 1945, and received a final package from him the following month.[35] Her parents' discussions never strayed from everyday matters or Himmler's fragile health; he was troubled for years by chronic gastric problems. "When I saw him for the last time, he said he hoped to return at Christmas, but couldn't be sure," she told the Allies.[36]

In April 1945, as American troops approached, Margarete and Gudrun left Gmund, heading south. The bunker Himmler had had built by Dachau prisoners was not going to be enough to protect them.

Fifteen-year-old Gudrun and her mother were arrested on May 13, 1945, in Wolkenstein, near Bolzano in South Tyrol. When General Karl Wolff, Obergruppenführer-SS and Himmler's chief of staff, was arrested in his sumptuous villa in Bolzano, he had made a deal with the Allies: "Let me return to Germany, and I will tell you where Himmler's wife and daughter are hiding."[37] Following their questioning, they were taken to luxurious lodgings in the home of a former film producer, where other female prisoners were being held. Next, they were transferred to a hotel in Bolzano, where they waited for two days before being transported to Verona for one night and then to Florence by plane and under escort for their protection from any possible attack by the general public or by the opposition. One of their guards at the British interrogation center in Florence told Gudrun and her mother, "If you tell anyone your name is Himmler, they'll tear you apart."[38]

Their questioning began. Margarete built her defense on ignorance: her husband had never told her about his activities. A British officer reported that she shut herself up "in a provincial bourgeois mentality."[39] Gudrun knew little more: she learned about the war mostly from the Allies and the foreign press during her imprisonment.

Next, they were taken to Rome, where they were held at the Cinecittà, Italy's largest motion picture studio, where an internment camp and intelligence office had been established. Himmler's wife and daughter were the only female detainees there, so the Allies had to construct a cell for them on the set of a Fascist propaganda movie. After four weeks, Gudrun began a hunger strike to protest the foul rations. Her condition quickly deteriorated and she began running a high fever. The British commander, known as "Bridge," sought the help of Hitler and Mussolini's interpreter to reason with the girl. Gudrun held out, and mother and daughter were served from the officers' mess thereafter. They were transferred subsequently to prisons in Milan, Paris, and Versailles, where they stayed for three days, before arriving at Nuremberg. "From now on, my name is Himmler. No more aliases, no more disguises,"[40] Gudrun declared. Her questioning at Nuremberg would prove fruitless: she knew nothing. When she was asked if she ever discussed the war with her father, she answered: "With my father, I never spoke of the war or anything like that."[41]

Gudrun still did not know what had become of her father. Her mother let it be known that she had a weak heart, leading the officers at the internment camp to withhold the news that her husband had committed suicide a few days previously on May 23, 1945, during a medical visit and strip search following his capture by British forces. After declaring, "My name is Heinrich Himmler," he had bitten a cyanide pill he had been concealing in his mouth. Although his stomach was pumped immediately, he died twelve minutes later.

On July 13, 1945, the United Press journalist Ann Stringer interviewed Margarete. She confirmed she knew of her husband's activities as the head of the Gestapo; she was proud of her husband, she said, and scolded the journalist: "In Germany, no one would dare ask a wife such a question." As for the world's hatred for the chief of the SS, she concluded impassively, "No one likes a policeman." When Stringer informed her of her husband's capture by the British and his suicide, she showed neither emotion nor surprise; she merely folded her hands in her lap and shrugged her shoulders. Stringer said she had never been face-to-face with anyone so cold:

"But even when I told her that Himmler was buried in an unmarked grave Frau Himmler showed no surprise, no interest. It was the coldest exhibition of complete control of human feeling that I have ever witnessed. . . . Then I asked if she knew what the world had thought of him and she replied, 'I know that before the war many people thought highly of him.' Frau Margarete denied the possibility that her dead husband might have been considered the No. 1 war criminal. She said, 'My husband? How could that be when Hitler was Fuehrer?' . . . Then pressed as to whether or not she was still proud of Himmler when he had sentenced millions of innocent people to death by torture, gassing, or starvation, Frau Margarete answered noncommittally, 'Perhaps. Perhaps not. It all depends.'[42] It is impossible to feel any sympathy for her."

Under questioning at Nuremberg on September 26, 1945, Marga Himmler confirmed that Heinrich always carried poison hidden on his person; many Nazi officials did the same and this was in compliance with orders from their hierarchy. She also stated that she discussed the war with her husband but denied that the concentration camps were ever a topic of those discussions: "I never had any knowledge about them. I have only just learned of their existence." When Colonel John Harlan Amen, the United States Army Intelligence officer who served as the chief interrogator at Nuremberg, inquired why she never asked Himmler about the camps, she answered: "I don't know."

He continued his questioning: "You knew that he was building them in certain places, isn't it true?"

She replied, "Yes, I knew that some of them existed, but I don't know who told me. I don't remember. Maybe it was him; I knew they had been built." After her initial denial, Marga finally admitted she knew that her husband was in charge of the camps and revealed that she had even visited the women's concentration camp at Ravensbrück. Nevertheless, she maintained that she was unaware of what went on there until she read about the camps in the newspapers in 1945.[43]

It was not until an interview that her mother gave to an American journalist on August 20, 1945, that Gudrun learned by chance of her father's suicide by poison before he could be interrogated.[44] The shock made her physically ill; she lay on her cot for almost three weeks in a delirium with a high fever. Gudrun had convinced herself that her father had been assassinated by the Allies; it was impossible for her to admit that he had killed himself. At that point, the British officer whose responsibility she was had had enough and began looking for a way to get rid of his troublesome young prisoner. However, no other officer wanted to have the Himmler girl in his charge, since she was of no use to the Allies and her security was a difficult matter. The only solution he found was to change her name; she would continue her life as Gudrun Schmidt, but not for long.

During the denazification campaign, and until November 1946, Himmler's wife and daughter were interned at women's camp 77 at Ludwigsburg. When the commander of the camp offered to release them, Margarete refused. She had no money, feared an assassination attempt, and had no idea where to go. They were finally admitted, under the diagnosis "feebleminded," to the Bethel Institution, a diaconal hospital for the mentally ill founded by the Pastor Friedrich von Bodelschwingh. The Protestant nurses tried to establish a rapport with Gudrun, but she remained aloof, declaring over and over "I want to be like my father," in other words, Catholic. Himmler had been, in fact, a fervent Catholic in his youth. He had drifted away from the Church eventually but he prayed every evening with his daughter. The nurses never saw Gudrun laugh or cry during her time at Bethel. She and her mother left the hospital in 1952.

What do we know of the world when we are just twenty years old? At the age of twenty, Gudrun still had not developed any emotional or critical distance from her adored father who had remained convinced until the end that he was a moral individual. Nazism, which is based on the concept of "pure" versus "inferior" races, made this logic possible, even in the face of what is universally understood as moral. However, when she learned of the crimes committed by her father, Gudrun could no longer use the skewed principles of the Third Reich as an excuse.

In 1947, her application to enroll in a fashion and design school was rejected outright on the basis of her name. When she was asked what her father's profession was, she had answered matter-of-factly: "My father was the Reichsführer-SS."[45] She was admitted the following semester after the local head of the Social-Democratic Party intervened, arguing that she should not be punished for the crimes of her father: "Our young democracy does not make children suffer for the sins of their parents."[46] She studied dressmaking and apprenticed as a seamstress. In 1950, when she was twenty-one years old, she left her mother and moved to Munich where she began looking for work. Once she learned she had a half sister and a half brother, she tried to contact them, unsuccessfully. Himmler's mistress, Hedwig Potthast, blocked her attempts.

Little is known about Hedwig's life after the war. In the 1950s, she left Bavaria and went to live in a village near Baden-Baden in the Black Forest, near one of her friends, Sigurd Peiper, formerly a secretary in the office of the Reichsführer-SS whose husband had been imprisoned for war crimes. Hedwig remarried and took her husband's name. Even less is known about her children; they lived in total anonymity. All that is known is that Himmler's son lived with his mother his whole life because of health problems while the daughter became a doctor. Hedwig Potthast died in Baden-Baden in 1994.

Every time Gudrun had to declare her family name, she was immediately sanctioned, denied employment or lodgings. Her colleagues and clients all refused any contact with a "Himmler." Yet, she was adamant about keeping her name.

In 1955, she traveled to London where she attended a party organized by Oswald Mosley with Adolf von Ribbentrop, the son of Hitler's foreign minister. When she returned, she let it be known with some pride that she had met a number of Fascists there. Her loose tongue cost Gudrun her job at the boarding house where she worked on the shores of Lake Tegernsee. When a client learned that the young receptionist was the daughter of Heinrich Himmler, he objected: "How could you let me be waited on by this girl when my own wife was gassed in the ovens at Auschwitz?"[47]

Her little apartment on the Georgenstrasse, on the outskirts of Munich, was a veritable museum to the glory of her father. Paintings, curios, decorations, busts, photographs: she lived surrounded by the many objects she had collected beginning in childhood. She had searched all over Europe as well, sometimes with the help of former Nazis who had kept relics. She found work as a secretary and led a simple life dedicated to the memory of her loving and affectionate father, whose participation in one of the greatest atrocities of history she could never admit.

She defends him tirelessly, unable to draw a distinction between her loving father and the SS monster, the blinkered fanatic, the architect and overseer of the Final Solution. She firmly believes that evidence will one day come to light that will exonerate him. The irrefutable proof that others have presented to her proves nothing. Can the particular bond she had with her father explain her willful blindness? It is difficult to form an opinion because she has never spoken on the subject. She gave only one interview, to the journalist Norbert Lebert in 1959.

Some years later, Lebert's son, Stephan, published that

interview and others conducted by his father in the book, *Denn du trägst meinen Namen.*[48] He argues that children such as Gudrun who prostrate themselves to the former glory of their fathers draw assurance from their hero worship. These children are powerless to admit the crushing burden of their families' histories. Of Heinrich Himmler, Gudrun only knew the good paterfamilias; the other aspects of his personality were only stories she read in the newspapers and in books. The only way forward for these children is to negate secondhand information, no matter how factual it may appear. To act otherwise would be a betrayal. Moreover, the repeated rejections Gudrun suffered during her life perhaps led her to consider herself a victim of injustice, just as she believed her father was.

In 1951, Gudrun joined *Stille Hilfe für Kriegsgefangene und Internierte* (in English, *Silent Assistance for Prisoners of War and Interned Persons*). It was created by Princess Helene Elisabeth von Isenberg, with the help of her contacts in the nobility and the Catholic Church, out of a perceived need to come to the aid of prisoners of war and interred prisoners, whom von Isenberg believed had been deprived of all rights. Under the direction of the lawyer Rudolf Aschenauer, the association provided legal aid to those accused of war crimes, whether they were held in prisons maintained by the Allies or detained in German jails, while their trials played out after the war. Von Isenberg thought of herself as a mother to the Nazi criminals held in the American prison in Landsberg, in Bavaria, where Hitler was a prisoner for nine months in 1924, and wrote *Mien Kampf.*

In 1952, Gudrun also helped found the group *Wiking-Jugund*, or Viking Youth, modeled on the *Hitlerjugund* youth organization of the Nazi Party. The group was banned in Germany in 1994.

The hard-core network of Stille Hilfe consisted of twenty to forty members and a hundred or so sympathizers. The association also provided aid to war criminals on the run: Adolf Eichmann, Johan von Leers, and even Josef Mengele would take advantage of these Nazi exfiltration networks, referred to as "rat lines" by the Allies. With the unfailing support of Stille Hilfe's members, they were all able to escape to South America. Klaus Barbie, known as the Butcher of Lyon, would also be helped by the association.[49] Oliver Schröm and Andrea Röpke, the authors of *Stille Hilfe für braune Kameraden: Das geheime Netzwerk der Alt-und Neonazis*, point out that the organization not only aids former members of the National Socialist Party but also officially collects funds for the neo-Nazi movement.

When journalists have questioned Gudrun about these activities, she has always given the same terse answer: "I never talk about my work; I just do what I can when I can."[50] Her work for the association included helping Anton Malloth, who was the Oberscharführer-SS at the Theresienstadt concentration camp; he was one of its cruelest and most feared guards and was undoubtedly in close contact with her father. For over forty years, Malloth lived undetected in Merano, Italy, before being extradited to Germany in 1988. Procedural failings left his case unresolved until 2001, when a Munich court delivered a life sentence. During all those years, Gudrun was his leading advocate. Stille Hilfe obtained a room for him in an upscale retirement home that had been built on land that had once belonged to Hitler's Deputy Führer, Rudolf Hess. In 1990, when it became publicly known that the German social security system (paid for by the German taxpayer) had footed most of the bill for Malloth's care in the home, the news was met with general consternation, much of it directed at Gudrun

Himmler. Loyal and undeterred, however, she continued her bimonthly visits to him, until his death in 2002.

Gudrun's isolation is not wholly by choice: society has no tolerance for her defense of her father or her own positions. Her involvement in organizations that aid former Nazis and her support of Germany's political far-right movement demonstrate that she means not only to rehabilitate her father but to pursue his gruesome ideals as well.

In the 1960s, Gudrun married a Nazi sympathizer, the writer Wolf-Dieter Burwitz, a Bavarian civil servant. He was accepting of her family history and subscribed to her father's beliefs. They live in Fürstenried, a Munich suburb, in a big white house. The couple has two children, one of which, a son, is a tax lawyer in Munich.

In 2010, Stille Hilfe also tried to block an extradition request by the Netherlands regarding a Dutch Nazi, Klaas Carel Faber. A Dutch court had pronounced him guilty in 1947 of the murder of twenty-two Jews and resistance fighters during the war.

Gudrun also became a militant for the National Democratic Party, a far-right ultranationalist political party in Germany, and she seems to enjoy her celebrity at meetings such as the Nazi gathering in Ulrichsberg in northern Austria. Perhaps she has concluded that, no matter what she does, she can never escape her past. If her reasoning is correct, rejecting the past would change nothing: her card has been dealt. As her father probably did before her, she has chosen to avoid any questions of morality, another way of avoiding her psychological burden. Is it possible that Himmler's daughter has never felt the tweaks of conscience? Even her great-niece, Katrin, has admitted feeling guilty "in some inexplicable yet distressing way."[51]

Guilt can sometimes skip a generation. Katrin Himmler's

in-laws are a Jewish family who survived the Warsaw Ghetto, and when she became a mother, she decided to write about her family history in a book entitled *Die Brüder Himmler*.[52] She had learned of the atrocities committed by the Nazis when she was younger, but, like many Germans, she had found it too painful to examine her own family's role. She has written that when it comes to condemning close family members, the psychological obstacles are too strong: "It is an uncomfortable process, constantly accompanied by fears of the loss it might bring."[53] In light of the very different choices she has made compared to those of her great-aunt, she maintains no contact at all with Gudrun Himmler.

In the case of children, those mental blocks are even stronger. Gudrun Himmler's most pertinent characteristics are her complete lack of objective distance from her father figure and her active role in the perpetuation of National Socialist ideals. For her, paying homage to her father goes hand in hand with supporting the Nazi ideology.

EDDA GÖRING

The Little Princess of
"The Nero of Nazi Germany"

It is a summer night in the port city of Hamburg in the late 1970s. Opera music is playing while an elegantly dressed group sips cocktails; their style is from another era and the music reminds them of their glory days. They are guests on a splendid vessel, a testament to the supremacy of German naval ship-building and a floating museum to Nazi Germany. The notes are from the Prelude to Act III of *Parsifal*, the last opera of the great Richard Wagner, the Third Reich's favorite composer. When the ship still belonged to its former owner, over forty years earlier, the same opera played then. Now, however, the music can hardly be heard over the voices of the guests, who pay it no attention. They are too busy remembering the best days of their lives.

The *Carin II* is a magnificent, eighty-nine-foot wooden yacht with the elegance of a royal cruise ship. That was, in fact, its intended purpose, when it was renamed the *Royal Albert* and served England's royal family for some fifteen years after the war—that is until its true identity was discovered and the family decided to sell it. Emmy, the widow of the yacht's original owner, immediately demanded it be returned to her, and her price was not cheap.

Among the guests on board, a large man stands out. His thinning blond hair is combed to one side over his high forehead, and thick square-framed glasses hint at his failing eyesight. He likes to be the center of attention and he loves anything that sparkles; he reminds some of the passengers of the ship's first owner, for those who once knew him, a man so tall he could barely squeeze his imposing frame into the ship's shower without becoming stuck there.

One woman sits by herself near the bow. Her name is Edda, and she stands out as much by her beauty as her identity. A solitary figure, she seems to inhabit the world only to maintain the memory of her father, for whom her love remains as unflagging as it is unconditional. He is the former owner of this yacht, Hermann Göring, and the most important man in her life. In 1937, the German automobile industry offered him this colossal gift, valued at 1.3 million reichsmarks (about 8 million dollars today). The ship was christened for his first wife, Carin von Kantzow, a Swede who died in 1931 at the age of forty-two. Edda often vacationed on this monument to her father's adored first love, and some of her most cherished childhood memories were made there. Photos in her family albums show her next to her father in the exact spot where she is seated tonight: he is wearing a yachting cap while she is laughing hilariously. Back then, he docked the yacht on Lake Wannsee, between Potsdam and Berlin. He loved to sail for hours on Potsdam's lakes and canals and he hosted sumptuous dinners on board that flowed with excellent wines and cognacs. There was even a platform that made it possible to hunt ducks, which were then served on board.

The boat's current owner is one Gerd Heidemann, a journalist at *Stern*, one of postwar Germany's largest news magazines. He is also a former member of Germany's state security service, the Stasi, and a Nazi apologist. Above all, he is a man who feeds on recognition and glory. He first discovered the ship while preparing a story on private yachting in 1972, but he had no intention of buying it then. He would reverse that decision one year later, taking advantage of the proceeds of the sale of his house and a favorable payment scheme, and in the hopes of reselling it to an American buyer. But he would change his mind yet again; the *Carin II* would be his vehicle to wealth and fame, no matter the price. Obsessed by the yacht's first owner, he would make it into a museum piece, replicating exactly its former decor by buying back much of its original fittings: silver and place settings, ashtrays, pillowcases, uniforms, etc. For five years, he would even be the suitor of Göring's only daughter.

The glory he sought so avidly would never come, however. A few years after this dinner, he published Hitler's private diaries, dating from 1932 to the Führer's death in 1945: seventy-two black-leather volumes carrying an embossed "FH" in the lower right-hand corner of each cover. Their last-known whereabouts had been a plane that crashed near Dresden in 1945. However, the "Hitler diaries" were no more than forgeries. Historians who were asked to authenticate the journals immediately expressed doubts, but the profits *Stern* stood to make were too huge to resist; the magazine brushed aside any attempt to declare them forgeries and published extracts as quickly as possible. Adolf Hitler became the hottest thing in publishing: *Stern*'s sales went through the roof and the foreign press, led by *Paris Match* magazine, fought to acquire publishing rights. *Paris Match* succeeded and ran the story on its cover, but the German police closed the party down when it revealed that the materials used in the notebooks dated from after the war. A forger named Konrad Kujau had written and sold them over a three-year period, with Gerd Heidemann's help, for 9.3 million deutschmarks. The story is one of the greatest scandals of German publishing, and Heidemann received a multiyear prison sentence.

But on this May evening in 1978, the night air is warm despite a cool breeze, and the guests are happy to gather, just like in the old days when Goebbels, Himmler, Heydrich, or even the Führer himself might have joined them as the guest of honor.

Seated among them, however, are other emissaries of the Third Reich—Himmler's aide-de-camp Karl Wolff; and Wilhelm Mohnke, the Kommandant of the Führer's bunker. The story of Hitler's final moments thrills the guests, and the alcohol that flows freely sharpens their nostalgia, but Edda, the "little princess of Nazi Germany's Nero" seems far away. She is the daughter of the Reichsmarschall Hermann Göring.

Edda was born on June 2, 1938. Her mother, the second wife of the commander in chief of the Luftwaffe, was Emmy Sonnemann, a provincial actress at the German National Theater in Weimar. Her parents had met in that city in 1932, when Hermann Göring had accompanied Hitler there. It was love at first sight for Emmy, who congratulated herself on her luck, declaring, "I am happy to have met a man, Hermann, who meets my expectations."[1] Their wedding in 1935 reflected Göring's taste for everything opulent and ostentatious; it could have been the coronation of an emperor.

Emmy Göring's sudden rise in status was ridiculed by her former friends at the theater. They called her sarcastically, "the grand lady," and the opera singer, Helene von Weinmann declared: "My God, Emmy is such a show-off. I knew her before she was a 'grand lady' and could be 'had' for a cup of coffee and 2.50 shillings."[2] Weinmann was immediately slapped with a three-year jail sentence; when she was released from Stadelheim prison in 1943, she was on her deathbed.

Hermann Göring became a father for the first time at the age of forty-three. Emmy announced the birth to him by telephone, sending all my congratulations, mine and little Edda's." He was ecstatic, rushing to her bedside and declaring Edda the most beautiful child he had ever seen. This reversed his earlier decision to wait a few days before meeting his daughter; everyone had told him newborns were hideous! To celebrate the birth, Göring led a squad of five hundred Luftwaffe planes on a flyover in the skies above Berlin. If Emmy had given him a son, it would have been a one-thousand plane flyover.

Edda's father was a decorated World War I fighter pilot who had received Germany's highest military honor, the *Pour le Mérite* cross. After the death of Wilhelm Reinhard, one of the famous Red Barons, Göring was named commander of the celebrated Flying Circus, an elite squadron.

He was one of Hitler's earliest lieutenants; nothing excited him more than power and its privileges. The creation of the Gestapo and the first concentration camps, including Oranienburg, near Berlin, were some of his contributions.

Rumor has it that Hermann Göring wanted to name his new

baby after Mussolini's favorite daughter, Edda Ciano. Edda
Göring has insisted that the name came from German mythol-
ogy, which both of her parents loved, whereas Emmy claimed
it was the name of one of her friends. Edda loved to remind
people that, "Farah Diba, the wife of the Shah of Persia, only
received 16,000 telegrams for the birth of the crown prince,
whereas when I was born, my parents received 628,000!" She
was baptized November 4, 1938, at Carinhall, Göring's hunting estate northeast of Berlin. The religious ceremony took
place with great pomp and circumstance, a fact that irritated
certain members of the Nazi Party, which included many anti-
Church radicals at the time. But with the Führer as the godfather, what good did it do to complain? A portrait of Edda in
the arms of her loving father sold by the millions throughout
Germany, and she received many presents, including one from
the city of Cologne, a painting of *The Madonna and Child*, by
Lucas Cranach the Elder whose work Göring admired. The
gift would later become the subject of a dispute between Edda
and the city of Cologne that lasted nearly fifteen years.

The Görings' family life was organized entirely around the
new child, whom they affectionately nicknamed "Eddalein."
She was the sunshine of her parents' lives. The star child soon
inspired jokes and anecdotes, so central a figure was she in
German life:

"Did you hear the Reichsautobahn has been closed to
traffic?"

"No, why?"

"Edda is learning to walk."

In 1940, the Nazi propaganda newspaper *Der Stürmer*
reported that Edda had been conceived by artificial insemi-
nation and was not Göring's daughter.[3] The accusation rested

on one fact—that Emmy Göring was already forty-four when she became pregnant—and one rumor—that Göring had been rendered impotent by a bullet wound he took in the groin during the famous Beer Hall Putsch in 1923. The British ambassador to Berlin himself was credited with telegraphing this information in 1936.[4] An enraged Göring demanded that Walter Buch, the Nazi Party regulator and a jurist, bring a lawsuit against *Der Stürmer's* publisher, Julius Streicher. This quasi-pornographic publication was the organ of vulgar anti-Semitism, but its sales had been steadily growing since 1935.[5] It was only after Hitler's intervention that Streicher was saved from Göring's claws and allowed to continue to publish his rag from his farm near Nuremberg.

Carinhall, named also after Göring's first wife, was the symbol of his power. Carin herself was there. Göring had his beloved wife's corpse brought back from Sweden in a monumental pewter casket and inhumed on the property. Built in 1933, about thirty miles from Berlin, the imposing lodge was as big as a castle and designed by Werner March, who would also design the Olympic stadium in Berlin. The building underwent two renovations in 1937 and 1939, which increased its size considerably. Still, nothing was too big, nothing too beautiful for Göring, who spent the Reich's money by the fistful, while failing to pay his workers. His reason: Carinhall was an official residence, the "House of the Reich." Hitler quipped that if you compared Göring's hunting lodge to his own mountain chalet, the latter would look like a lowly gardener's hut.

Edda grew up with Carinhall as her extravagant home, surrounded by immense grounds and, beyond that, thousands of acres of forest where bison, buffalo, deer, elk, and wild horses roamed freely. The rooms were stuffed with all of the artwork

Göring pillaged in his insatiable treasure hunting: he liked to think of himself as the Reich's greatest patron of the arts.

The mansion's basement was equipped with a cinema, a gymnasium, a pool, a billiards room, and a Russian steam bath. Elsewhere on the property were medical examining rooms, a bunker and a reception hall, called the *Jaghalle*, or hunting hall, measuring over three thousand square feet. It was lined with hunting trophies and featured a church's nave heated by an immense fireplace. For leisure activities, as if the hunting and other distractions were not enough, two thousand feet of electric train tracks, worth $268,000, had been laid in the attic. Lion cubs were also on the property, raised solely for the delight of the family and visitors. In the interest of safety, they were replaced every year by the Berlin Zoo when the resident cubs reached one year of age. The Görings raised seven cubs in all, and all were hand-fed with a baby bottle. Edda delighted in watching her father play with her favorite cub, Mucki, and even Mussolini liked to have a tussle with the little lion when he came to visit. Yet another of his fantastical ideas was a weight-loss machine that he liked to demonstrate for the Duchess of Windsor. By this time, his fighter pilot's physique was a distant memory. The dashing and muscular officer who liked to call himself Iron Man weighed 320 pounds in 1933. The American ambassador to France, William C. Bullitt, joked about him, "He is at least a yard across the bottom as the crow flies . . . two inches of padding extending each [shoulder] . . . nearly a yard from rear to umbilicus . . . and encases himself in a glove-tight uniform, the effect is novel."[6]

Not only was Göring an immoderate collector of jewels, he also loved to dress up in different outfits; and was known to change clothes as many as five times a day. His guests might discover him in a Roman toga or an emperor's robe or carry-ing a spear. He wore makeup, red nail polish, and diamond rings, and in these accoutrements he did not hesitate to parade around in front of a transfixed Albert Speer or a mesmerized Hans-Ulrich Rudel, a famous pilot.

Speer met him in 1943 as the Nazis' fortunes began to turn, and he recorded later his "astonishment" to discover a "rouged" and "lacquered" Göring in a green velour dressing gown pinned with an enormous ruby, who "occasionally scooped a handful of unset gems from his pocket and playfully let them glide through his fingers" while they talked.[7] The Italian foreign minister, Galeazzo Ciano, noted in his journal in 1942, seeing Göring in a fur coat "such as a high-class prostitute would wear to the opera."[8]

The little princess was the adored child of a proud father who spent all of his spare time with her, playing, dancing, or cuddling. He loved to show her off in elaborate staging. There is one photo in which Edda is posed in a reed basket in front of Carinhall, facing an audience of admirers, among which is her father, seated in the front row. When Emmy wanted to employ a nanny, a Nazi official rebuked her for not hiring a party member. She replied that she did not belong to the Nazi Party, nor did any of the members of her family. Hitler solved the problem immediately by assigning her the number of a deceased party member.

Edda lived her earliest years in the lap of luxury, surrounded by loving, attentive parents who considered nothing too perfect for the princess. She had a tutor and lived isolated from the rest of the world, removed from the privations of the war, according to her mother's biography.

For some welcome distraction, the Luftwaffe, commanded

by Göring himself, offered her a miniature replica of Frederick II's palace in Potsdam. The King of Prussia's castle became Edda's dollhouse, complete with kitchens, drawing rooms, and figurines, even a theater with a stage and curtains.

She did meet a number of historical figures whose mark on history would prove more or less honorable: Herbert Hoover, the Duke and Duchess of Windsor, the pilot Charles Lindbergh, Benito Mussolini, the kings of Bulgaria and Yugoslavia, Willy Messerschmitt, and Ernst Heinkel, among others.

Edda's life was a daily fairytale. Göring never went to bed without kissing his adored Eddalein good night. He began to remove himself from political life and devote more and more time to his daughter.

Corrupt and devoid of any initiative, Göring was harshly criticized by Hitler. In the late 1930s, Hitler assailed him for his weak leadership of the Luftwaffe, and Göring fell irreparably from grace when it lost the air war. Hitler called him "the greatest failure,"[9] and the Allies nicknamed him "The Fat One." Under the effect of narcotics, a euphoric, beady-eyed Göring could launch into a rant lasting several hours at a time, then finally lose steam, rest his head on the table before his stunned guests, and fall immediately into a deep sleep.[10]

At her fourth birthday party, Edda wore a tiny red Hussar's uniform, made just for her by the costumers at the National Theater. In a photo taken that day, she stands at mock attention in perfectly polished little leather boots. At the age of five, she began piano and classical dance lessons. For her sixth birthday, on June 2, 1944, her godfather the Führer presented his gift in person, with a declaration intended for her father: "Just you wait and see, Göring! The greatest victory of the century is going to be ours!"[11] For her last Christmas before

Germany's defeat, her mother gave her six pink nightgowns cut from bridal silk from the Reich Chancellery.[12]

This luxurious life far from the horrors of war ended on January 31, 1945, the day Edda and her mother were forced to flee the advancing Russian army and seek shelter at Obersalzberg, near the Austrian border in Bavaria. Seven years in the life of a princess ended forever the moment the door of Carinhall closed behind her.

As the Red Army approached, Göring himself ordered the property to be dynamited. After transferring his art collection—worth more than two hundred million reichsmarks—to Berchtesgaden by special convoy, he let a demolition team from the Luftwaffe take care of the job. As he rose through the ranks, he had freely indulged his all-consuming passion for art. He brought to Carinhall paintings, tapestries, jewels, statues: "gifts" he extorted from Germany's cities and business community. He was never beneath letting it slip that he would be only too happy to be made a gift of "such and such" piece of art at one of the Reich's society events. He also shamelessly pillaged the occupied countries of Western Europe and dispossessed many Jewish art collectors. His appetite was insatiable.

In Paris, the Jeu de Paume Museum was one of his favorite hunting grounds. He personally selected everything he wanted sent to him in Germany. His looting allowed him to boast later, "At the current moment, thanks to acquisitions and exchanges, I possess perhaps the most important private art collection in Germany, if not all of Europe."[13]

On April 20, 1945, the Führer's birthday, Berlin was burning and all roads leading south, including to Berchtesgaden, were cut off. Hitler had decided to shelter in his bunker in

Berlin. Göring, believing himself Hitler's successor and wanting to leave the city as quickly as possible, let it be known that a high official of the Third Reich needed to be transported to safety in the south, and he hurried to make preparations for his departure, requiring his usual full makeup, a white silk uniform, and forty-seven monogrammed suitcases.[14] In Berchtesgaden, everyone worried if he would make it, particularly his wife and daughter. Germany was falling to the Allies, but the Göring family was reunited on April 21.

On April 22, Göring believed his moment of glory had arrived. A decree signed on June 29, 1941, had designated him as Hitler's legal successor in the event the Führer resigned as commander in chief of the military. He wished to have Hitler's consent before taking such an extraordinary step, but his plan was foiled by Bormann, the powerful secretary of the Nazi Party, who had already convinced Hitler that Göring was a traitor. In fact, when he arrived in Berchtesgaden on the evening of April 21, he had already been stripped of his right of succession.

Göring was arrested on April 23 by the SS acting under Hitler's direct orders: "Surround Göring's villa and arrest immediately the former Reichsmarschall. Crush any resistance. Adolf Hitler."[15] The house became a prison, with guards posted in the hallways and staircases. All communication was cut off, and Hermann, Emmy, and Edda were confined to their rooms.

The end came quickly. On April 25, Göring received a telegram from Hitler, written by Bormann: "Hermann Goering, Obersalzberg. Your action represents high treason against the Fuehrer and National Socialism. The penalty for treason is death. But in view of your earlier services to the Party, the Fuehrer will not inflict this supreme penalty if you resign all your offices. Answer yes or no."[16]

As the Allied air strikes began nearing Obersalzberg, the family was led into the basement and then into deep underground tunnels. Göring was kept separate from the others, and no one was allowed to communicate with him. The intensified bombings terrified the little girl, who cried uncontrollably, but the conditions underground—in dark rooms crudely excavated from the limestone rock some one hundred feet underground—were equally terrifying. Her father was not allowed to come to her, the tension was thick, there was no ventilation, and the lack of oxygen made it impossible to even burn a candle.

Göring agreed to resign, and Hitler stripped him of all responsibilities within the Party and banned him from it as well. Radio Hamburg announced his resignation on April 26, citing health reasons. Göring tried to reassure his wife and daughter, whom recent events had completely taken by surprise. Emmy was convinced that Bormann, Göring's sworn enemy, was plotting an assassination attempt. The couple decided to send a message to the Führer: if he truly believed that Göring had betrayed him, he should execute the entire family, Edda included.[17]

In a letter addressed to Germany's Ministry of Special Affairs in 1947, Emmy virulently objected to the measures used to detain her and Edda. They had been arrested in their nightgowns, subjected to the cold, and nearly shot by the SS when an aide-de-camp had simply tried to hand them blankets.

Emmy Göring reported overhearing the following conversation between Edda and her nanny, Christa, on the subject of Emmy's adored godfather, Adolf Hitler:

"Edda: I don't like it when people say bad things about my godfather. Whom do you like better, Christa, my Uncle Adolf or my daddy?

Christa: Your daddy.

Edda: You have to love Uncle Adolf, too.

Christa: No, I don't; he wasn't good to your daddy.

Edda: That's impossible because my daddy loves him, too!"[18]

When the bombing ceased and the family came out of hiding, they discovered that most of Obersalzberg, including their own house, had been destroyed.

Several days later, taking advantage of a reduced police surveillance during a change of guard, Göring fled Berchtesgaden for the medieval castle where he had spent his childhood. This was Mauterndorf, in Austria, which he had inherited from his godfather, Hermann von Epenstein in 1939. The family was together again, but not for long. The castle was hardly welcoming, with its thick walls, glacial interior, and rumors of hauntings, but Edda saw her father regain his composure and she too felt reassured. Emmy, however, was inconsolable, distraught by the knowledge of everything they had lost and she wondered out loud every night she tucked Edda into bed whether they would live to see another day.

On May 1, 1945, the news of Hitler's suicide was broadcast around the world. On May 7, with Göring's liberation order signed, the family attempted to reach Fischhorn Castle near Zell am See, Austria, but was discovered by the US Thirty-Sixth Infantry Division, led by Brigadier General Robert I. Stack. The Görings were allowed to spend a last night together in the castle before surrendering the following day.

A military aide present that day later reported he would never forget the sight of the little girl in the back seat of the sedan, sobbing as she watched her father arrested. The family had been allowed to spend the morning in the comfortable second-floor apartments of the chateau. Göring took a long bath and then went downstairs to have his photo taken in front of the Texas flag.[19] On this day, May 9, 1945, his wife and child did not yet realize they would never again see him a free man. Göring had sent several letters to Dwight D. Eisenhower, the Supreme Allied Commander in Europe, requesting to meet with him, and he was convinced the general would grant him an interview and find him a way to save his skin. The man who would become the thirty-fourth president of the United States decided differently, however. The time had come to strip Göring of his marshal's staff and his medals and treat him like the prisoner of war he was.

Edda celebrated her seventh birthday on June 2, 1945, for the first time without her father. The family was temporarily separated. On June 20, mother and daughter were relocated, at their request, to Veldenstein Castle; although these new lodgings were empty and unheated, they belonged to Göring, who had purchased the castle from his godfather. Five months later, Emmy and Edda finally received news from Hermann, who was under arrest in Augsburg. A family photo arrived, delivered by US Army Major Evans, and bearing a message in Hermann's handwriting, "I trust Major Evans completely." Edda wrote him back, "To my adored papa!! We are at Veldenstein now. I miss you terribly, terribly, and I love you so much. Come back to us soon. . . . The pansies smell so sweet and the roses are so pretty. I pray to God every night for us. 1,000,000 kisses from your Edda!!!"[20] She sent him the note with a drawing of an Easter egg, a house, and spring flowers, as well as a photo of herself. Göring was forbidden to receive mail, however, and he would never read her note.

After initial questioning in Bavaria, Göring was transferred to Camp Ashcan in Mondorf-les-Bains, Luxembourg, on May

22, 1945. He carried 280 pounds on his five-foot-six-inch frame
and was doped up on Paracodeine; he had been addicted to morphine ever since the 1920s to relieve the pain of his many injuries, particularly those sustained during the Beer Hall Putsch in
1923. At first, he took daily morphine shots; later, Paracodeine
pills. His attempted detox and the several weeks he had spent
in an asylum when he lived in Sweden had not cured him. In
prison, although he had been taking between twenty and forty
pills daily, he was forced into withdrawal. Colonel Burton C.
Andrus, the commander at Mondorf-les-Bains, remembered
their first meeting: "When Goering came to me at Mondorf,
he was a simpering slob with two suitcases full of Paracodeine
pills. I thought he was a drug salesman."[21]

Although his detox would last the first few months of his
imprisonment, he remained focused on trying to meet General
Eisenhower.

Joachim von Ribbentrop, Karl Dönitz, and forty-nine other
high-ranking Nazi officials were waiting at the camp to be
transferred to Nuremberg the following September. Their only
pastime consisted in watching documentaries about the Nazis'
crimes.

On October 15, 1945, Emmy Göring was arrested at Veldenstein and imprisoned at Straubing, ninety miles from Nuremberg. She was separated from Edda without knowing where
the girl would be taken. The girl was sent to a neighboring
village and would join her mother in prison seven weeks later.
She arrived with her teddy bear and a suitcase of clothes for the
bear, under an escort of American soldiers who did not speak a
word of German. She knew she was going to be reunited with
her mother but she must have been terrified.

The press described Emmy as "Straubing's star prisoner" and relished her downfall from "First Lady of the Nazi Reich" to "haggard political prisoner of the US Army, who has to clean her own cell and wash her own clothes."[22] She was not allowed to receive mail, and she remained without news of her husband. Edda would later say about their stay in Straubing, "Actually, I found it comfortable there."[23] She slept in her mother's cell on a straw mattress covered by a checkered blanket that, as rumor had it, had been given to her by Mussolini. There were some happy moments; on December 6, 1945, a fellow prisoner disguised as St. Nicholas brought her chocolates.

When mother and daughter were freed in February 1946, they were penniless and had nowhere to go. Like Margarete and Gudrun Himmler would do when offered their freedom, Emmy and Edda Göring asked the prison director to let them stay.

Fifteen days later however, in March 1946, it was time for them to leave Straubing. An American journalist, Peggy Poor, found them lodgings in a small hunting chalet in Sackdilling, fifteen miles from Nuremberg, near Neuhaus, in exchange for an interview with Emmy.

The chalet belonged to a forest warden by the name of Frank. His wife had known Göring as a young man; in fact, Göring himself had the chalet built and used it to change and rest after hunting parties. The journalist left for Nuremberg the following day to inform Göring that his wife and daughter had been released.

Emmy and Edda took daily walks in the surrounding forest. Emmy was Edda's teacher as well, helping her learn her multiplication tables and teaching her literature. In their reduced straits, they could no longer afford to keep Edda's tutor but the family of Carin, Göring's first wife, would support them financially.

Göring's lawyer was able to petition for his client to send and receive mail, and Göring was relieved to communicate again with his wife and daughter. Emmy remained bitter, despite her newfound freedom. In interviews, she confided, between sobs, how the Americans had unfairly treated her. In her version of events, she was a destitute woman who had been robbed by the SS of £8,000 and a fur coat, even though they knew she would need it. She accused the Americans of dispossessing her of artworks valuing £50,000, leaving her with just bare essentials. In tears, she told one reporter, "Do you know . . . when we moved here from Austria the Americans allowed us to bring only one car for me and little Edda . . . and all our belongings."[24]

Emmy could not understand how her husband's complete loyalty to Hitler had been rewarded with an order for his arrest and assassination; Hitler might even have been prepared to have Edda murdered, his own goddaughter. In her mind, Göring's loyalty was immoderate, the kind of legends in the *Nibelungen-lied*.[25] When a messenger who had visited Emmy and Edda on March 24 brought Göring news of his wife's state of mind and her desire to strip him of his delusions about Hitler's treatment of him, the prisoner refused to listen; Emmy could sway him in certain matters but not on this. Some fundamental principles were beyond the understanding of mere women.[26]

For his daughter's eighth birthday, on June 2, 1946, Göring wrote her a letter, "From the bottom of my heart, I pray to God almighty to watch over you and help you."[27] He included a card for his wife, in which he sent her his "passionate love."

"Nazi Number One," as Göring liked to refer to himself, was formally charged in the Nuremberg trials that were held between November 1945 and October 1946. In early September, Emmy was informed that she could visit her husband, after a seventeen-month-long separation. Visits were limited to thirty minutes and prisoners were separated from visitors by glass and bars.

Edda was not allowed into the prison. As a minor, she could only visit on Children's Day, held on September 18, although the same conditions applied for child visitors, meaning she could neither touch nor kiss her father. Emmy told her not to appear sad in front of her father, to which Edda replied, "Don't worry, Mother." She saw her father for the last time on September 30, 1946. Göring's right hand was manacled to his guard so he raised his left hand and pronounced this blessing over his wife and daughter: "I bless you and our daughter. I bless our dear country. And I bless anyone who will help you in any way."[28]

At his trial, Hermann Göring entered a "not guilty" plea, as did all of the other senior defendants at Nuremberg. Emmy saw him a final time on October 7, 1944, and told him, "You can die in peace knowing you did everything you could at Nuremberg. I will always think of you as having died for Germany."[29]

In his last letter to his wife, Hermann told her, "My life ended the moment we said goodbye for the last time. . . . In his goodness, God spared me the worst. All my thoughts are with you and Edda. . . My heart will beat to the last for our great and eternal love. Your Hermann."[30]

When Edda learned of her father's death sentence, she asked her mother innocently, "Is Papa really going to die?" And when Hermann asked Emmy if Edda knew he would be executed, she explained that she chose not to lie to the girl because Edda needed to trust her mother completely. It was her duty to tell her the truth and she hoped that the girl's life would not be too difficult.

At the end of their visit, Emmy asked Hermann, "Do you really believe they are going to shoot you?" Göring responded in a firm voice, "You can be sure of one thing—they won't hang me. No, they won't hang me!"[31] He was under the illusion that one day he would be remembered as a martyr for Germany and that "in fifty or sixty years there will be statues of Hermann Goering all over Germany."[32]

Found guilty on all four counts, including war crimes and crimes against humanity, and sentenced to death, Hermann Göring committed suicide on October 15, 1946, several hours before he was to be executed by swallowing a cyanide pill that had probably been supplied by one of his American guards. His daughter thought an angel must have descended through the ceiling of his cell to give it to him.[33]

Heinrich Himmler's suicide spared him a trial; Göring's spared him an execution.

On May 29, 1947, Emmy was arrested at her house in Sackdilling. Like all the wives of important Nazis tried at Nuremberg, she was accused of having profited from the Nazi regime. She was afflicted with sciatica and had to be transported by ambulance. Despite her mother's reassurances, Edda, who was nine, believed her mother was also going to be sentenced to death. Emmy was placed in a former work camp for Russian women in Göggingen near Augsburg. Over one thousand women were held there in five low barracks; Emmy insisted that "as the wife of Hermann Göring [she] was entitled to special treatment."[34] Her demand was ignored. On October 31, 1947, she wrote to the competent authorities:

"May I explain my case to you and petition for help? I was brought to the women's internment camp at Göggingen, under orders by the previous minister Loritz. I was in bed at home with severe sciatica pain and phlebitis in my right arm. I have suffered from sciatica for the last thirty-five years. The doctor treating me objected to my being moved. . . . Nevertheless, I was put on a stretcher at midnight and driven here for seven hours, because I supposedly tried to escape in the English zone. . . . I have been bedridden here for the last five months with intense pain . . . I am fifty-four years old and I have been through so much these past years. . . . Dear sir, perhaps you are familiar with my case: I was completely apolitical, I helped people who were persecuted for racist and political reasons when and where I could, there is sufficient formal testimony on this subject. My one fault is that I was the wife of Hermann Göring. It is unthinkable to punish a woman because she loved her husband and was happy with him."[35]

At Christmas, Edda was authorized to spend two days with her mother. Thereafter, she was allowed one monthly visit. On July 20, 1948, during her denazification trial, Emmy was charged by Julius Herf, the prosecutor for special affairs in Bavaria, in whose eyes she was a prime suspect. Although she had always described herself as apolitical, she admitted under questioning that, as Göring's wife, she had always shared her husband's ideological positions. She claimed complete ignorance of the concentration and extermination camps and defended herself from accusations that she had lived in a state of ostentatious luxury. Emmy Göring justified everything on the grounds that she loved her husband. "I always considered love to be a blessing; I never knew you could be punished for it."[36] The prosecutor reminded her that she had created a scandal when she attended a performance at the Vienna opera house wearing a white ermine coat and expensive jewels. Her trial lasted two days. Fifteen witnesses testified in her favor and she had the support of the well-known actor Gustaf Gründgens and the pastor Jentsch, who argued in her defense that she had provided aid to numerous Jews. Nevertheless, Emmy Göring was convicted as a beneficiary of the Nazi regime. She was sentenced to one year in a work camp, was banned from exercising a profession for five years, and was fined 30 percent of her remaining property. Since she had already served her prison sentence, she was released at the close of her trial, which led to a public outcry.

In 1948, when Edda was ten, she left her mother and aunt, who were living in Hersbruck, for St. Anna, a girls' school in Sulzbach-Rosenberg, Bavaria. This was the beginning of her formal schooling; until then, she had had a private tutor during the war and then Emmy had taken over her education. Upon learning who Edda's father was, the school director was initially reluctant to offer her a place but felt she could not refuse such a brilliant student. Edda graduated in 1958; one of the essay topics on her final exams was, "Is forgetting both a blessing and a danger?"

In 1949, she was faced for the first time with a dispute over ownership of some of her property when her mother initiated legal proceedings for the restitution of certain gifts which, she claimed, had been offered to Edda by her father or by "admirers, with the best intentions in the world, I don't know who." At the heart of the suit was the *Madonna and Child* painting by Cranach the Elder. The assistant public prosecutor for Bavaria, a Dr. Auerbach, argued that these gifts had been made "to curry favor with her illustrious father."[37] A suit was subsequently brought against Edda by the office of denazification.

Edda began law studies with the intention of becoming a lawyer, but she found the program dull and dropped out, although she did graduate from the University of Munich. Like Gudrun Himmler, she is steadfast in her love for her father and refuses to believe he was one of the architects of the Shoah. Edda is convinced he had no role in the persecution of the Jews, despite the fact that in July 1941, he ordered the SS general Reinhard Heydrich to devise a plan for carrying out the Final Solution in Europe.[38]

On the question of Göring's guilt, Edda and her mother had come to the same conclusion, and the two women shared a tiny apartment in Munich until Emmy's death in 1973. Mother and daughter made the apartment into a shrine to the man who, if he had not entered politics, might have become a chocolate maker, like his grandfather. "If only he could have been content making chocolate bars, we would all be together today and happy," his daughter mused.[39] In 1967, Emmy decided to write her memoirs to "set the record straight." Even though she was fully aware of the extent of the Nazis' crimes and the millions of people they had murdered, her Hermann was only kindness, love, and selflessness.

Like Gudrun Himmler, Edda has placed all the blame on Hitler. Göring will always be her "wonderful father." "My father was not a fanatic. You could see the peacefulness in his eyes. . . . I loved him very much and you could see he loved me."[40] Proud to be her father's daughter, she wears her name with pride, believing it comes with more advantages than disadvantages, particularly when she travels. "When people learn I am Göring's daughter," she has said, not without a hint of arrogance, "waiters refuse to let me pay the check, taxi drivers won't even tell me what I owe for the ride," and she is often introduced to the local dignitaries wherever she goes.

The daughter of the Third Reich's strongman became a nurse in a hospital laboratory in Wiesbaden, Germany. She remains in touch with Winifred Wagner, the wife of the son of Richard Wagner and an old friend of Adolf Hitler. Emmy Göring shared her husband's love for Wagner's music and has said that Edda inherited it, too. After the fall of the Reich, Winifred Wagner was fired from her post as director of the Bayreuth Festival; Richard Wagner had been its first. In the 1950s, Winifred, who had never renounced her past, began to become involved in different far-right associations, at whose meetings she came in contact with Edda Göring, Ilse Hess, and Oswald Mosley, the leader of the British Union of Fascists. Florentine Rost van Tonningen, the "Black Widow" apologist of National Socialism in The Netherlands, confirmed in an interview that Edda has remained a supporter of the neo-Nazi ideology and participated at times in demonstrations.

Some troubling parallels exist between the daughter of Himmler, that narrow-minded bureaucrat and mastermind of the Final Solution, and the daughter of Göring, who was Nazism's Nero. Both women continue to adore their fathers, denying the evidence of their crimes. Both have lived or live still in Munich in homes they have made over into museums dedicated to their fathers' glory. They also share this in common—they both refuse to speak to journalists. A foreign correspondent for the French newspaper *Le Monde* reported how it went when she tried to contact Göring's daughter in the 1990s. Edda answered the phone by giving her full name as is the German custom, but when she learned the purpose of the call—a story on the children of Nazi leaders and the collective memory of the Shoah—Edda firmly refused to participate: "I don't give interviews." She took a moment to explain herself, however. "I never encountered any problems because of my name. On the contrary, it's a source of pride. . . . My father is still a popular figure in Germany. The media won't admit it but what they report doesn't reflect public opinion. The Bavarian government made us suffer, my mother and I, but the Bavarian people, they always supported us." Her response was spontaneous, unguarded, and showed the extent of her feelings, her anger, and her bitterness. As if she realized she had revealed too much, she refused to say any more. "No interview," she repeated, adding only, "I love my father very much; that, at least, you can write."[41]

As in the Himmler family, the burden of the past has been visited on a later generation: Göring's great-niece and her brother. In their thirties, both made the choice to be sterilized, so as to avoid bringing another Göring, another monster, into the world. Bettina Göring lives on the other side of the Atlantic Ocean, in New Mexico, far from society and "off the grid." She thinks she resembles her great-uncle even more than Edda does. She remembers the Reichsmarschall as someone so frightening that he made everyone else in the family, which included some ardent Nazis, seem insignificant. Once, when she was eleven, she was watching a documentary on the concentration camps with her grandmother, who told her, "It's all a pack of lies!" In the Göring family, as in many homes all over Germany, it was much simpler to deny any personal involvement. No one was to blame for anything, not even Hermann Göring.[42]

As for Göring's great-nephew, Matthias Göring embraced

the Jewish faith. When he turned forty, he began wearing a kippah and a Star of David, eating kosher, and keeping the Sabbath. After his physical therapy practice went bankrupt in the 2000s, his wife left him, and Matthias, depressed, began to contemplate suicide. He prayed for help and believes God told him to visit the Holy Land. He went to Israel and lived with a community of Holocaust victims. But he denies his conversion was a response to a repressed guilt. "I don't feel guilty. Our family and the German nation have a spiritual guilt, and it is our responsibility to recognize that openly. I think that God took the opportunity to use my name to change certain things in people's hearts."[43]

Edda Göring remains steadfast in her convictions. In 2015, at the age of seventy-six, she filed suit against the Bavarian parliament to return some of her father's property that had been confiscated after the war. Her suit was immediately rejected.

WOLF R. HESS

A Life in the Shadow of the Last of the War Criminals

He has decided to say nothing to his son. The boy is much too young, and his mission is top secret. On this day, unusually, he has taken a few hours to play trains with the child, after which he holds him tightly in his arms before handing him to his nurse, who will put him to bed. He knows without a doubt that this is the last time he will ever see him. He has hidden letters to his family, as well as his will, among the toys, just in case. Before leaving, he puts a photo of his beloved son in the inside pocket of his coat.

His plan is to tell Churchill that Germany will not threaten Great Britain's empire if, in return, England does not attempt to block Germany's actions elsewhere. He will go alone, as he was instructed in a dream; the moment has come to meet his destiny. What prompted him to take this peace offer directly to the English was a series of visions he has had of "an endless line of children's coffins with weeping mothers behind them."[1]

Up until now, he has stayed in the shadows, but no longer: now will he reestablish his influence over "the Man" whom he worships before anyone else: the Führer.

To carry out his mission, he has visited Willy Messerschmitt at his hangar in Augsburg and explained to him that he wants to learn to fly a Bf 110 fighter plane. Thereafter, an unregistered aircraft has been held in reserve for his personal use, after having been outfitted to his specifications: the plane is disarmed and has long-range fuel tanks with a flight radius of over 2,500 miles, or ten hours of flight.

He has trained for months, waiting for his moment and keeping an eye on the weather. Poor conditions have prevented him from taking off on several occasions.

But on this Saturday, May 10, 1941, at 17:45 MET, the Messerschmitt Bf 110, radio code VJ+OQ, finally takes off from the Augsburg airfield, abut forty miles from Munich.

The Luftwaffe would be conducting a night raid on London that same day; the pilot knows his mission is perilous and that, once in the air, there is no turning back. He has carefully studied the aerial maps, however, and knows his flight plan by heart. He has circled in blue where he intends to land, in the north of England; in Scotland, precisely.

The sky is clear and the night is beautiful above Germany. He is wearing a new Luftwaffe uniform. He considers himself a messenger of peace and wants to look the part: this is not a mission to conduct in civilian clothes. Before boarding the gray Luftwaffe bomber, he gave his adjutant a letter with orders to deliver it to Hitler four hours after his departure.

Cruising through German airspace, his mind races. He is convinced he is fulfilling his destiny and carrying out the wishes of the Führer, who will certainly be grateful. "If I pull this off," he thinks, "history will thank me and I will be worthy of the Führer, who wants this peace as much as I do." He remembers the dream that convinced him to carry out his plan, a mission that has become an obsession and his destiny.

He is Rudolf Hess, the Deputy Führer.

After flying nearly one thousand miles—over four hours—solo from Bavaria, Hess entered British airspace at the Farne Islands at 22:05, keeping the plane at very low altitude, between thirty-two and fifty feet. Near Edinburgh, the Royal Corps of Signals detected him but Hess kept flying. The Royal Air Force unsuccessfully attempted an intercept, then lost sight of him. In fact, Hess had changed direction and was flying inland from the British coast, toward Glasgow.

At 23:00, believing he had reached his destination at Dungavel House, the residence of the Duke of Hamilton, the pilot parachuted out of the plane for the first time in his life, and landed in a field near Eaglesham, about twelve miles from Dungavel. He injured his ankle in the fall and was arrested around midnight. The British were intrigued to find his maps, on which the Duke of Hamilton's home was clearly circled, and the business cards of a certain Karl Haushofer, which Hess brought to facilitate an introduction with the Duke. Hess was identified early the following morning by the Duke, and Hess was hopeful that he would welcome the idea of a peace treaty with Germany.

When Hitler read Hess's letter, delivered by his two aides-de-camp, and realized the extent of Hess's plan, he asked the famous fighter pilot and head of the Luftwaffe's engineering department, Ernst Udet, if such a mission could succeed. "Impossible!" was the answer. Even under favorable weather conditions, a biplane would never reach the coast of Scotland; crosswinds would prevent it from landing in England and it would be pushed out to sea. Udet was proved wrong.[2]

Rudolf Hess was born April 26, 1894, in Alexandria, Egypt, into a family of wealthy German merchants. His early childhood was spent in a veritable palace with domestic staff. He was close to his mother, Klara Munch, a loving woman whom Hess loved greatly in return. During his imprisonment at Spandau in 1949, he referenced this quote from the German philosopher Immanuel Kant: "I shall never forget my mother. She implanted in me and nurtured the first seed of good; she opened my soul to the lessons of Nature; she aroused my interest and enlarged my ideas. What she taught me has had an everlasting and blessed influence upon my life." He added, "This holds true not just for the mother of Kant."[3] Rudolf Hess stayed in close contact with his adored mother his entire life. His father was a strict, puritanical merchant who did not tolerate insubordination; his wish was that his son would take over the business and he therefore directed him into an appropriate course of studies. But Rudolf's only desire was to leave.

His escape route would be through the military. At the outbreak of World War I, Hess was twenty and began pilot training. When he saw Hitler speak for the first time in April 1920, he had a vision, he would later say, in which he saw "the Man" who alone could set Germany back on its feet to stand again with pride.

By the following July, Hess was the sixteenth member of the Nazi Party; it would take several years for its ranks to swell to the 8 to 8.5 million it would later count. Nothing about timid Rudolf predestined him to become Hitler's deputy or the

third-ranking official of the Reich; nothing except his unswerv-
ing loyalty to the Führer. He liked to say that he thought of
himself as the Party's Hagen, referring to a great warrior from
the *Nibelungenlied*, whose unfailing loyalty to his king knew no
bounds. Hess was the very picture of subservience to Hitler; his
wife remembered there was an almost "magical" bond between
the two men.[4] Rudolf Hess became Hitler's right-hand man
for all matters concerning the Nazi Party, but this was perhaps a calculated move to remove Hess more easily if and when
necessary. His detractors called him Hitler's lapdog, and his
own power-hungry chief of staff, Martin Bormann, easily sup-
planted him in the Führer's favor.

Rudolf also met his wife, Ilse Prohl, in 1920. Ilse was
a student living in the same boarding house as Hess in the
Schwabing section of Munich. The couple married on December 20, 1927, but struggled for ten years to have a child. They
explored different alternative therapies and consulted all kinds
of healers; both were fanatical believers in occult science.
Magda Goebbels remembered how "Frau Hess had told her for
five or six years in succession that she was at last going to have a
child—generally because some prophet had predicted it."[5] Her
husband liked to consult Tarot card readers and fortune tellers.

A close associate of Goebbels remembered "Goebbels spoke
of Hess's mental illness and then described the comedy of Hess
and his wife, who had been trying for years to produce an heir.
No one knew for sure whether the child was really his. Hess was
alleged to have gone with his wife to astrologers, cartomanc-
ers, and other workers of magic and to have drunk all kinds of
mixtures and potions before they were successful in begetting
a child."[6] Felix Kersten, Himmler's masseur, also remembered
finding Hess lying in bed with magnets suspended over and

under his mattress; Hess had explained that he was following a magnetism treatment to eliminate "harmful substances" from his body.[7]

Ilse was unhappy with the physical changes of pregnancy, especially when she had to meet the Duchess of Windsor, whom she idealized as the most elegant woman of the century. She was uncomfortable in her body and in public. She hoped the child would be a boy, but objected to the possibility that he might follow his father into politics, believing that the father always overshadowed the son in such situations.[8]

When Wolf Rüdiger, the long-awaited son, was finally born, November 18, 1937, Rudolf was forty-three. Childbirth was long and difficult for Ilse, but the important thing was that the long-awaited child was finally there. Hess was with Hitler at his mountain lodge, the Berghof in Berchtesgaden. News of the birth filled Hess with joy and he beamed one of his characteristic smiles, looking half blissful, half crazy, as only he could. Hess had a rather unusual physiognomy, in fact, coupled with the air of a fanatic, with deep-set eyes, high cheekbones, and thick eyebrows.

The couple's choice of name for the child combined the nickname Hitler had taken for himself after years of political battles, "Wolf," and the name of a hero from the *Nibelungenlied*, the Nazis' favorite saga, "Rüdiger." The new parents were strong believers in astrology, and Ilse was convinced her son was born on an auspicious day, when the stars had aligned. The night before his birth, the moon had been full, and the child was born under the influence of Jupiter, Mars, and Venus.[9]

A naming ceremony was held, inspired by pagan ritual, since baptisms were outlawed under the Nazis. Two godfathers were designated: Hitler and Karl Haushofer. The latter was

Hess's professor of geopolitics at university, as well as his mentor and a close friend.[10] Gifts were sent from all over Germany, and the order had been given to all of the Nazi Party's regional leaders, the Gauleiters, to send a small bag of earth from their regions. Hess placed the dirt under the infant's crib, believing it symbolized the beginning of his son's life on German soil. Ilse had always been careful to preserve the couple's privacy and she was more determined than ever to keep her son safe from the world outside. She insisted that Rudolf curtail his absences, fearing that the child would fail to create a bond with him and would have to readjust to his presence at each homecoming. Hess obliged, spending as much time at home as he could. He was immensely proud of his son and convinced he was destined for greatness; even the shape of the boy's ears was interpreted as a sign of his potential "musical genius." His parents put the child to bed at night with classical melodies and woke him in the morning to jazz, but he never showed any musical talent.[11]

Wolf Rüdiger was only three and a half when his father shocked everyone by flying solo to Great Britain in the hope of signing a "separate peace" treaty. This failed endeavor, which spawned speculation of all kind, remains one of the mysteries of the twentieth century. Certain British documents about the flight on May 10, 1941, remain classified; many unanswered questions linger. No one in Hess's entourage was aware of his plan. Ilse had seen his weather bulletins and maps and suspected that something was afoot, but ignored what it could be. She thought it might be a mission to France for a meeting with Marshal Pétain, but England? Never.[12] She was equally surprised that evening to find him dressed in the blue shirt and dark tie of the Luftwaffe uniform and his pilot boots, an outfit that inspired her respect but which he never wore anymore. Hess had been a skilled pilot, but a reckless one too, leading Hitler to ground him. When she inquired when he would be home again, he responded he would return the following Monday, but his answer did not convince her. Did the Führer know about Hess's plans? Did he approve? These questions remain unanswered. However, for Wolf Rüdiger, there was never any doubt in his mind: Hitler was aware of the mission. He spent his life trying to establish his conviction as truth.

The truth, however, is not so simple. It seems that Hess devised his plan in the belief that it was what the Führer wanted. Hess had helped Hitler write *Mein Kampf* when they were imprisoned together at Landsberg, and he was convinced that Hitler would have wanted to maintain an entente with England. Some evidence for this argument can be found in the fourteen-page letter that Hess wrote Hitler and had delivered to him after he left, in which he explained his reasons for the flight and for attempting to meet the Duke of Hamilton. Hamilton also loved aviation and Hess believed him to be an enthusiastic Germanophile. Hess himself always denied Hitler's involvement in the plan, and Göring agreed under testimony: "Hess is insane. He's been insane for a long time. We knew it when he flew to England. Do you think Hitler would have sent the third man in the Reich on such a lone mission to England without the slightest preparation? Hitler really blew up when he found out. . . . If he had really wanted to deal with the British . . . my own connections with England were such that I could have arranged it within forty-eight hours. No, Hess took off without a word, without papers, without anything. Just left a crazy note behind."[13]

Following his arrest in England, all of Hess's direct

collaborators were jailed, and the Nazi press reported he was afflicted with a mental condition. Hitler declared that if Hess ever returned to Germany, he would send him either to a psychiatric hospital or before a firing squad. There were rumors he suffered from an illness that had attacked his brain. The governor-general of occupied Poland, Hans Frank said, "According to the Führer, it is evident now that Hess was entirely under the sway of astrologists, iridologists, and healers."[14] Claiming amnesia, whether real or feigned, Hess remained imprisoned in England until October 1945, when he was transferred to Nuremberg. Acute paranoia and increasing madness was the diagnosis delivered by the psychiatrists who examined him. He preserved samples of his meals in prison in the hope that tests would one day prove the Allies had attempted to poison him, and several times he discreetly switched meal trays with a superior officer on the belief that his food contained some dangerous substance. During his imprisonment at Nuremberg, Hermann Göring commented on Hess's behavior in prison. "If the coffee is too hot, he thinks he is being targeted by an attempt to burn him. If it's too cold, he thinks it's a ploy to anger him. He doesn't say that exactly, but that's the gist of everything he says."[15]

Rudolf Hess's fall from grace forced his wife and son to leave their home in Munich where Wolf was born and to retreat to their summer house, the *Bürgle* in Bad Oberdorf. Wolf Rüdiger would claim later that Martin Bormann, who replaced Hess as the Führer's secretary, was the cause of their troubles. Eva Braun, Hitler's mistress, rather agreed and supported the family, encouraging them in a letter: "Don't hesitate to let me know if there is anything you need, I'll speak to Hitler when Bormann is absent."[16] Wolf Rüdiger understood her comment as proof of Bormann's nefarious influence on Hitler. Before long, Hess's name was no longer spoken in Germany, and his photo was removed from walls and schools. Streets bearing his name were renamed. The little boy was too young to understand the extent of the scorn heaped on his father, although some of his friends distanced themselves and his parentage sometimes came back to haunt him.

Rudolf Hess was happy his son was becoming a "mountain boy." Bad Oberdorf lies at an altitude of 2,750 feet at the top of the Iller Valley in the Allgäu Alps, a beautiful alpine region famous for its picturesque mountain landscapes. On October 21, 1941, Rudolf received his first letter from Wolf Rüdiger, who was four years old, an experience that saddened him deeply; reading the boy's words and seeing his childish manuscript led him to wonder if he would ever see his adored son again. News from his wife and son, whom he nicknamed "Buz," was the source of his only happiness in prison. He was relieved to learn that his beloved child had not forgotten him and he took a special interest in the boy's education. He sent the boy advice, encouraged him to speak well, and taught him chess. When his son announced he wanted to drive a municipal garbage truck in Munich when he grew up, his father asked him to consider driving trains or planes instead. Nonetheless, the difficulties posed by this long-distance education frustrated him, and father and son both suffered from their forced separation. So began Wolf Rüdiger's life in the shadow of his loving, absent father of whom he retained only a few memories such as his father's comforting voice the day a bat flew into their house, and his father playing with him in the yard of the house in Munich.[17]

As the years passed, however, the memories faded and the

photos yellowed; the image he kept of his father in his mind's eye blurred. He held him in the highest respect and defended a man who, unlike Hermann Göring and his boundless greed, never used his power to enrich himself. Hess wrote from prison in 1945, "One thing only I wish for my son: that he becomes possessed by something! I don't care what it is: inventing machines, a new discovery in medicine, or the drama—even if nobody ever makes the machines, the play is never acted or even read, or the doctors of all opinions, united for once, fall upon him to tear his notions to bits."[18] He also deplored the fact that the Allies censored all of his correspondence, which he considered a violation of the family's privacy.

Hess was not found guilty of crimes against humanity at Nuremberg but he was given a life sentence for crimes against peace. After the trial, one of Wolf Rüdiger's classmates told him he was lucky. "Be happy, your father won't hang."[19] Wolf Rüdiger was only eight at the time, and the sentence came as an enormous shock; he would never understand it and could never accept it.

His punishment was simply unwarranted in the eyes of a son who believed his father was a martyr for peace, not a criminal. He concluded the trial was a travesty of justice. Hess's final statement at the trial, before the verdict was delivered, made a lasting impression on the boy. "I regret nothing. Were I to live my life again I should act once more as I have acted now, even though I knew at the end that a funeral pyre was already flickering for my immolation."[20]

Hess would never renounce his fanaticism or his anti-Semitism. For Rabbi Abraham Cooper, assistant dean of the Simon Wiesenthal Center in Los Angeles: "A life sentence for this unrepentant Nazi is an act of compassion in comparison with the fate suffered by the millions who were redefined as subhuman by a stroke of Hess's pen."[21] After nine months at Nuremberg, Hess was transferred to Spandau Prison with six other detainees. Spandau was a red-brick fortress with capacity for six hundred prisoners, but it would house only these seven Nazi defendants. The conditions were difficult, prisoners were often kept in solitary confinement, and Hess refused to see his family for twenty-four years.

Fortunately for Wolf Rüdiger, or Buz as he was called, his father's identity and crimes were of no concern to the other children living in Bad Oberdorf. Once however, another child taunted him, "Your father was a Nazi!" Not grasping the meaning of the insult, Wolf Rüdiger shot back, "So was yours!" To which the other replied, ending the argument, "Yours was a bigger one!"

The fact that mother and son lived alone did not arouse any suspicion in postwar Germany. Many children did not have fathers at home. On June 3, 1947, however, Ilse was arrested and detained with the wives of other Nazi officials, including Emmy Göring, Brigitte Frank, Henriette von Schirach, and Grete Frick, at Augsburg-Göggingen. Ilse Hess was assigned to Barack V, cell 5. On June 7, 1947, she wrote to her husband, "I have good luck, since I seem to have been placed in the most friendly room that has been known here for a long time. . . . We are commanded by the oldest inhabitant . . . with a deep masculine voice . . . [and who] smokes like a chimney."[22] In another letter, she described the bravery of little Wolf, who was nine, during her arrest. As soon as he saw the police, he hid himself in the pantry to cry. Ilse was released on March 24, 1948, and, following her denazification trial, was stripped of all of her property.

Wolf Rüdiger, who was in the care of his aunt Inge following Ilse's arrest, was allowed to join her in prison four weeks later. There, he was reunited with the children of other Nazi criminals, such as Edda Göring. He liked to steal away to the men's prison to listen to their stories and imagine he was a soldier like them. It was during this postwar period that he gradually discovered the role his father played in the rise of the Third Reich and of its crimes.

In 1950, Wolf was sent to a boarding school near Berchtesgaden but was brought home again after a scandal broke out concerning homosexual relations at the school. Ilse wanted to enroll him at the famous Schule Schloss Salem but the Margrave of Baden refused to have the son of the Führer's former deputy at this educational institution for Europe's elite. The only option left was to bring him back to Berchtesgaden where he attended the "Christophorus" parochial school. In September 1950, Hess wrote his son, "You can believe me when I say that to swallow an injustice silently, without flinching, although fully conscious that your conduct was completely right, can impart (to a man more especially) an inner freedom that cannot be shaken by anything."[23] In *Rudolf Hess: Prisoner of Peace*, published in 1950, Ilse published the entirety of their abundant correspondence after Rudolf's arrest. The couple used a kind of personal code in their letters; for example, a wavy line indicated the word "laugh." The British army at first believed this to be a secret code.

In 1955, Ilse opened a boarding house, The Bergherberg in Gailenberg in the Allgäu Alps. She would remain close to other National Socialism sympathizers as well as the organization in which Gudrun Himmler played an active role. She corresponded regularly with Winifred Wagner, the daughter-in-law of Richard Wagner, who maintained close ties to the National Socialist German Workers' Party. Wolf Rüdiger was raised in an environment where the Nazi ideology was never renounced: quite the contrary.

His school years passed unremarkably. After his graduation in 1956, he traveled in South Africa with a school friend. There, he discovered quite a different reality than what he had read about; he thought that racial segregation was intrinsically good, and white leadership a foregone conclusion.[24] While there, he contracted a tropical disease whose treatment, he would become convinced, was the cause of the serious kidney problems he developed a few years later.

It was at this time that he began to challenge the revelations in the media about the Third Reich, and particularly what was reported about his father, whom he still considered unjustly condemned. For Wolf Rüdiger, Rudolf's peace mission could only have been planned with the consent of Hitler, and he based his claim on both the close relationship between the two men and the four-hour meeting they had had just days before the flight. Moreover, after Hess was imprisoned in England, Hitler had arranged for Ilse to receive a pension. Wolf Rüdiger dismissed outright the theory advanced by some historians, that Hess had planned the mission himself in order to reassert his power over Hitler.

In 1959, he refused to be called for compulsory service in the Bundeswehr, arguing that his father was sent to prison as a cosignatory on the March 16, 1935, law creating a military draft, which was deemed a crime against peace at Nuremberg. He appeared before an examining commission on two occasions and, in response to a military physician who asked him which branch of the military he preferred, he answered that, if forced, he would rather serve in the mountain infantry. He wrote to the commission: "You will surely understand that my conscience forbids me from completing my military service to satisfy the same people who sentenced my father."[25] If they insisted with their order, he let it be known, they would have to arrest him. His requests were refused on insufficient legal grounds, but in 1964, he won his case as a conscientious objector. He enrolled at the Munich Technical University and became a civil engineer.[26]

His campaign to vindicate his father began in earnest in the 1960s. He used the media to portray his father as an ambassador of peace, a myth that his father and his father's lawyer, Alfred Seidl, began to circulate during the Nuremberg trials. Faced with the reigning "victor's justice," in Hess's opinion, this was his best angle of defense. Wolf Rüdiger created the Committee to Free Rudolf Hess and launched a petition that was signed by more than 350,000 people, including two former presidents of West Germany; Gustav Heinemann and Richard von Weizsäcker; two Nobel Prize winners, Otto Hahn and Werner Heisenberg; and the writer Ernst Jünger. Thomas Mann's son, Golo Mann, prefaced one of Wolf Rüdiger's books, arguing that Rudolf Hess was not a man of war. The easiest person of all to convince was, of course, his mother, Ilse.

On November 20, 1967, Ilse Hess granted an interview to the German newspaper, *Der Spiegel*. Twenty-six years had passed since she had seen her husband, the day he left home to fly to England. He had refused visits from his family during his imprisonment at Spandau, wishing to spare them the ordeal of seeing him in his reduced state. Ilse believed that his failure to carry out his plan had sent him into a depression but she refused to accept that he was mentally ill.

The medical community has never been in agreement as to his condition: depression, schizophrenia, and any number of other pathologies have been considered. "A typical schizophrenic," was the first impression of the psychiatrist who examined him immediately after his arrest in England, Major Henry Victor Dicks of the Royal Army Medical Corps. Dicks diagnosed a serious depressive state and paranoid schizophrenia. He also noted hypochondriac tendencies, observing that Hess had brought with him on his flight aspirin, laxatives, caffeine pills, barbiturates, antiseptics, methamphetamines, opiates, homeopathic medicines, and pills for motion sickness.[27] His suicide attempt was considered proof of his depressive state. Winston Churchill declared him to be utterly sane, however—Germany could have demanded his repatriation in the case of a mental illness—and he insured that the clinical reports were not released to the public. The American psychologist Douglas M. Kelley confirmed that Hess was "on the verge of a serious nervous depression"[28] during the Nuremberg trials and determined that Hess had developed a father complex on Hitler, after first seeking a father figure in his former professor and mentor, Karl Haushofer. Ilse thought that diagnosis was absurd, even false, and politically motivated. Hess also presented signs of amnesia that had to be proven real or faked. Colonel Amen, the chief interrogator at the trials, arranged a meeting between Hess and Haushofer on October 10, 1945, to prod his memory. The professor used the occasion to deliver news of Hess's wife and son. "Your son is very well. I saw him. He is a fine boy, and I said goodbye to him under the oak, the one that bears your name."[29]

In his prison cell in Great Britain, Hess kept three portraits above his bed: his wife's, his son's, and the Führer's. He took only the first two with him when he was transferred to Nuremberg. He would receive additional news of them from two of his former secretaries, who were also sent to jog his memory. Yet none of these meetings proved decisive for the psychiatrists tasked with determining whether Hess's amnesia was genuine or an act. Questioned about his wife and son, Hess claimed he had forgotten everything about them, even their names.[30] Only the photographs he kept of them seemed to have any effect on him. Nevertheless, he wrote them letters in which he addressed them by name, which would disprove his claims. Göring was convinced Hess had pulled a fast one on the court and his psychiatrists, and shared his delight with Hess. "Any doubts I had left me when you failed to recognize Haushofer at that confrontation."[31] There is one thing on which everyone can agree, however: he remained under the sway of his stubborn fanaticism until the very end.

In his letters to Ilse, Hess showed a close interest in his son's progress at school, devising veritable correspondence classes for him and encouraging his wife to teach Greek to the boy. He hoped Wolf Rüdiger had time for leisure activities that would distract him from the dull monotony of everyday life in Germany and expressed concern that he not grow up too fast. No photographs had been taken of Hess for years, and his face eventually became no more than a blur for his son, although it was captured once by a single photographer through the barbed wire at Spandau.

Unlike some of his fellow prisoners at Spandau, Hess never used his mental illness as grounds for requesting parole. He never allowed his lawyers to do so either, under the logic that such a defense revealed a weakness that was unbefitting of the Deputy Führer. In November 1969, suffering terribly from a duodenal ulcer, he finally asked the prison director if his wife and son could be allowed to visit him. The request was granted but any reference to or mention of politics or National Socialism was forbidden.

Wolf Rüdiger was thirty-one when he saw his father again in 1969. Hess was seventy-five. They were not allowed to touch each other in any way; father and son would embrace each other again only in 1982. They were never authorized to be alone together, either; one of the prison directors was always present. Finally, no gifts could be exchanged, even at Christmas. The first meeting took place on December 24, when Wolf Rüdiger was accompanied by his mother. He had a thousand questions for his father, but they would never be answered. Wolf Rüdiger dedicated his life to his father, writing three books: *My Father, Rudolf Hess* (1986), *Who Murdered My Father, Rudolf Hess?* (1989), and *Rudolf Hess: No Regrets* (1994).[32] Questioned about his own life, he would respond invariably, "I never had time for myself: I spent all my free time on my father."[33]

In *My Father, Rudolf Hess*, Wolf Rüdiger describes the conditions at Spandau and references the experiences of the French prison chaplain, Georges Casalis, regarding the inhumane treatment of the prisoners there.[34] For Wolf Rüdiger, Rudolf Hess was the loneliest prisoner the world has ever known; his monthly mail allotment consisted of one letter of less than thirteen hundred words, and the family carefully saved every one of them.[35] Rudolf and Ilse were even required to refrain from drawing a wavy line in their letters to designate a smile, as was their custom. Many other letters were found in violation of those rules and never arrived, leaving gaps of several months in their correspondence. Rudolf Hess received many photographs of his son, but complained to Ilse that he could not get a good look at him because of the angle or the lighting.[36]

In 1966, Hess became the only remaining Nazi prisoner at Spandau: Albert Speer, Hitler's chief architect and the Reich Minister of Armaments, and Baldur von Schirach, the leader of the Hitler Youth, were released in that year, whereas the four other prisoners, of the seven initially imprisoned with Hess, had been freed in the 1950s. As the only prisoner keeping Spandau open, Hess was the most expensive criminal in the world. His incarceration cost the German state 2.5 million deutschemarks annually.[37]

Throughout his father's imprisonment, Wolf Rüdiger worked tirelessly to secure his father's release and improve conditions for him. A ray of hope appeared in January 1987, when the Soviet embassy responded to his request. Until then, the Soviets had fiercely opposed any motion to free Hess on humanitarian grounds, since they would have been the principal victims of an Anglo-German peace agreement. However, the warming of East–West relations led to a softening of their position. A meeting was arranged for March 31, 1987, at 2:00 p.m. When Wolf Rüdiger went to see his father to discuss it with him, he found him considerably weaker and unable to walk on his own. Hess informed his son that he had finally submitted a request for parole, after forty-six years in prison, forty-two of which were spent at Spandau.

On April 13, 1987, the German newspaper *Der Spiegel* published an article entitled "Will Gorbachev release Hess?" Wolf Rüdiger was convinced that Hess's liberation was imminent. On August 17, 1987, however, a journalist telephoned him at his office to inform him his father was dying. He received another call late in the day from Harold W. Keane, the American director of Spandau, confirming his death. The official announcement was made in English. "I am authorized to inform you that your father expired today at 4:10 p.m. I am not authorized to give you any further details."[38]

When Wolf Rüdiger arrived at Spandau the next day with his father's lawyer, Alfred Seidl, a crowd was blocking the entrance. Wolf Rüdiger was convinced his father had been assassinated. He was met by a nervous Keane, who refused to let him view the body. The autopsy determined that Hess had committed suicide by hanging himself with an electric cord in the shed where he often went in the prison courtyard. After an unsuccessful attempt to resuscitate him, he was declared dead at 4:10 in the afternoon. He was ninety-three. The Allies' official report on the circumstances of his death was published a month later on September 17.

Wolf Rüdiger visited his father 102 times during his detention at Spandau. Despite the years of separation, he insisted that the emotional bond he had with his father remained as strong as ever. Following the death of the man who cast a long shadow over his entire life and for whom he spent his life fighting to defend, Wolf Rüdiger suffered a stroke and was hospitalized in Munich at the age of forty-nine.[39]

Spandau was demolished immediately after Hess's death to avoid its possible use as a Nazi heritage site. Following an agreement between the Allies and the Hess family, the body was not cremated but transferred instead to the family, who buried it privately in the family mausoleum in Bavaria.

Convinced that his father was assassinated, Wolf Rüdiger had a second autopsy performed in Munich when the body was returned to the family. The report, prepared by Wolfgang Spann, agreed that death had been caused by asphyxiation but also revealed the presence of bruises on the neck indicating strangulation. Two prison guards at Spandau also asserted that agents of the British Secret Service were at Spandau that day, with the consent of the CIA and under orders to kill Hess. Wolf Rüdiger also challenged the authenticity of an apparent suicide note found in Hess's pocket by the Allies; its closing statement, "written a few minutes before my death," sounded nothing like his father's style and its contents were out of date in 1987. Wolf Rüdiger concluded that the note was in reality a farewell letter his father had written twenty years earlier that was never delivered to him and his mother. He concluded beyond a shadow of a doubt that his father's death was the result of a British plot whose ultimate goal was to prevent Hess from setting the historical record straight upon his release from prison, a theory confirmed, in his eyes, by the fact that documents concerning Hess's detention in England remained classified until 2017. For Wolf Rüdiger, his father risked his life in the goal of peace and was a victim, not a criminal. Were he to become a martyr, he asserted, the Allies would only have themselves to blame; if they had freed him twenty years earlier along with Albert Speer, the world would have forgotten about him.

Wolf Rüdiger Hess never overcame his resentment about the imprisonment of his father, the messenger of peace whom he spent his life idealizing. He argued that the Nuremberg laws, of which his father was a principal cosigner, were only the German translation of the desire of Orthodox Jews to live separate from other religions. The laws were not racist in and of themselves, he claimed; the problem lay with their interpretation and implementation by a few Nazis. Wolf Rüdiger could not accept that his father participated in the mass extermination of Europe's Jews. He found support for his theories in the fact that his father's professor and mentor, Karl Haushofer, was married to a Jew and that Hess provided Haushofer with a letter of safe passage to protect him from the laws that he had himself created.

Finally, for Wolf Rüdiger, the invasion of Poland in September 1939 was a strategy to protect the German minority there, which the Poles were massacring by the thousands; Hitler had no choice but to attack Poland to avoid being encircled. Wolf Rüdiger swore on his father's writings as if they were Bible truth and could never rest until his theory regarding his father's assassination was accepted as fact. He was a bitter and hateful man who readily denied the reality of the Final Solution. He has been called a revisionist, a term he embraced, defining the role of a revisionist as "unmasking the falsehoods of what we Germans have been taught about our history."[40]

According to his line of thinking, Germany's one mistake was to sign the Treaty of Versailles. Hitler was neither a madman nor a monster. As was the case for the Third Reich generally, he was grossly caricatured, the victim of a senseless propaganda campaign that spread far-fetched myths about the number of victims of the war and their extermination. He dismissed the firsthand accounts of survivors, arguing that if anyone survived at all, the stories about the Nazis' atrocities could not be true. He also argued that the gas chambers were a technically impossible feat.[41]

Proud of his father to the end, Wolf Rüdiger also never considered his name a curse; quite the contrary was true. He shared Edda Göring's experience in this regard, believing that people loved and would continue to love his father: Rudolf Hess was the conscience of the Nazi Party, and his long prison sentence could only move his fellow Germans to feel greater sympathy for him.

Wolf Rüdiger's son, Wolf Andreas, was born on April 20, Hitler's birthday, a coincidence that pleased Wolf Rüdiger immensely. He gave the child the Führer's nickname from his early political years. The boy learned to admire his grandfather Rudolf, and his father boasted that little Wolf was very eager to learn more about this man whose significance he "grasped entirely."[42]

Wolf Rüdiger had two more children whom he raised in the same cult of Rudolf Hess, but little is known about them. Wolf Rüdiger died in 2001, after ten years of dialysis.

Right up until his death, he led the Rudolf-Hess-Gesellschaft e. V.,[43] an organization he founded in 1988 to rehabilitate his father's reputation, notably by lending credence to the theory that Hess was assassinated, an idea disseminated by a number of websites created for this express purpose. One of these websites was designed as a source of "unbiased" information about Hess's life and death, but has since been taken down.

Wolf Andreas is a computer programmer today. He had planned to create a website in honor of his grandfather but was fined in 2002 for having refuted on the Internet the existence of the gas chambers at Dachau, which he insisted were installed by the American army after the war to frighten tourists.[44]

In 2011, twenty-four years after the death of Rudolf Hess, his grave in the village of Wunsiedel in Bavaria, was secretly opened by the family, under orders by the mayor of Wunsiedel who wanted the body exhumed in order to put a stop to neo-Nazi commemorations, especially those marking the anniversary of his death. His ashes were scattered in the sea, but a silent march in his memory is held every year by Reich nostalgia seekers.

Just as Gudrun Himmler and Edda Göring did, Wolf Rüdiger Hess dedicated his life to writing his father's place in history as a martyr. Other Nazi children, however, were consumed by hatred when they learned the truth about their fathers' actions during the war. Niklas Frank was one of these. His father, Hans Frank, was the governor-general of occupied Poland and was sentenced to death.

Wolf Rüdiger Hess believed that Frank's son was mentally ill and declared his hatred for his father indecent. Niklas Frank pitied Wolf Rüdiger in return, believing that his life was irredeemably altered by the burden of Rudolf Hess's life sentence; "[F]rom that point of view things were harder for Hess's son than for me,"[45] he has said.

Niklas Frank

A Hunger for the Truth

"There, that's the corner, driver. Pull over! Such beautiful corsets they have! But no, first I'm going to look at the furs. Wait for me here. You too, Niklas. I won't be long."

By standing on the back seat of the black Mercedes sedan and angling his nose up to the rear window, four-year-old Niklas can just spy the three-foot-high barbed-wire walls of what in Kraków is sometimes called the Forbidden City. The tramway does not stop here, in the ghetto where the Jews have been contained. A grim scene meets his gaze, rattling his naive confidence in the world. He is pleased that his usually distant mother brought him along on her shopping excursion but he cannot understand the sinister picture before him. Death seems to be lurking everywhere; there are even corpses lying on the sidewalk.

His mother had told him once that the best place to buy a corset is in this sordid place. "No one makes better corsets than the Jews in the ghetto," were her exact words. He imagines that corsets must be very important; why else would anyone come here? He is not afraid, however; the driver and an adjutant are there to protect him and his mother. Anyone who dared to so much as even approach the car would be beaten to death or summarily shot. But who are these people? Are they even human? The Führer called them "vermin" and said they must be wiped out. Niklas shakes his head in confusion. The same "vermin" make the beautiful corsets that his mother will come to this desolate place to buy, dirtying her shoes in this quarter she reviles as "so *schumtzig*" (so dirty). Fifteen to twenty thousand Jews are trying to survive here, confined in such close quarters that lice and typhoid and all kinds of illness are rife.

How do these people live, he wonders? Even he can see that the poverty is shocking and the filth is horrifying. There are children outside the car window; some look as if they could be his age. Why are they here? They look afraid, and their clothes are ripped and soiled, when they have clothes. Some are half-naked and so skinny he can see their bones! There is snow on the ground, and they don't even have shoes! What have they done to be in such a broken-down place? Have they been punished? And their eyes: so big! Bigger than their faces! Don't they have anything to eat? He thinks about all the nice things he has at home to eat, even chocolate!

The children have seen him and are looking back at him now. It makes him uneasy. "Why are they staring at me? That boy especially, with a yellow star on his arm. Did I do something wrong? Is it the car they're looking at? What's going on?" He decides to make a face and sticks out his tongue mockingly. "Now he'll stop looking at me! Ha, like that! Good, that scared him. See how he ran off? I showed him!"

Ghetto: he has often heard the word at home and he knows that this is the place to come to get the lowest price on all kinds of things the Jews have. But why this is, he does not understand. When his mother returns to the car, he decides to ask her:

"Mother, why don't they smile? Why do they look at us with such hate?" And he adds, "It's Sunday after all, and they have a yellow star on their arms."

Niklas always wears lederhosen and a jacket on Sundays.

His mother brushes away his questions impatiently and tells him not to ask any more because he won't understand. This little boy is Niklas Frank, the son of Hans Frank, the Butcher of Poland.

He has never met a Jew. The meaning of the yellow star is a mystery to him. His brother Norman said there was once a Jewish boy in his class before the war but that he disappeared one day and no one bothered to find out where he'd gone. Norman is eleven years older than Niklas. Norman went to the ghetto once too, with his father and the driver. He thinks the ghettos were there before their family came to Poland. But he never understood why his father went to the ghetto either.[1]

Niklas always stays in the car while his mother, Brigitte, shops in the ghetto. Every time, she returns with jewelry, furs, rugs, and other valuable items, thrilled by the deals she has negotiated. It is the only thing that matters to her. The morbid silence and the indescribable misery she walks through has no effect on her whatsoever.

Once, Niklas was allowed to get out of the car to stretch his legs. Walking down a dark passageway, a particularly cheerless house caught his attention. He pushed open the heavy door to find a man yelling furiously at an old woman who was just skin and bones. She stared at the ground while he accused her: "You evil witch." The little boy was so frightened he burst into tears. The man told him, "Don't get so upset; she'll be dead soon." Niklas never forgot that scene. It would still haunt him when, years later, sitting in a room he kept purposely unheated, he would write his first book about his father, Hans Frank, on an old Erika typewriter that had once belonged to his mother.

When they arrived in Poland in 1939, the Franks took up residence at Wawel Castle—which once belonged to the Jagiellon monarchs—on the hills above Kraków, the capital city. His father commandeered this Renaissance castle for the family's personal use and he had a wing furnished in the style of the Third Reich. An enormous Nazi flag flew above its walls. That the Franks lacked for nothing was an understatement. The family lived in the private apartments on the second floor. The number of employees in their personal service was impressive, and Niklas, the little prince, lived in unheard-of luxury. More than seventy years later, he would remember the day his parents offered each brother a pedal car. Thrilled, Niklas immediately got behind the wheel of the nicer of the two, a miniature Mercedes . . . but his mother ordered him out, informing him that he was in Norman's car. He thought his car looked ordinary. It was a stinging realization.[2] Nevertheless, the two brothers never tired of racing their sports cars through the halls of the castle. Niklas would wait until one of the domestics approached, then pedal at full speed into the legs of the hapless servant. No one would dare reprimand the little prince, the son of the governor-general.

Many receptions were held at the castle, whose wine cellar was stocked with fine wines and French cognacs. Guests smoked Cuban cigars. Succulent dishes, chocolates, and fruit jellies were passed from silver trays. No one would ever have imagined that people were living in abject misery and dying of hunger just a stone's throw away.

It was not until after the war that Niklas learned of his father's role in the legalization of the ghettos, which were initially under the jurisdiction of the police. Hans Frank defended this policy, which he said was taken "in the interests of the Jews."[3] Niklas would write later that his mother "should have thanked Hitler for the ghettos, which she treated as if they were discount stores especially designed for the Frank family."[4]

Psychiatrists at Nuremberg testified that certain Nazi officials presented perfectly normal psyches that harbored neither fanaticism nor sadism, but this was not the case of Hans Frank. A versatile and tormented figure, he was an early and total convert to National Socialism. Right up until the end, he would prove a slavish vassal to Hitler, that "glorious genius in the art of ruling."[5] He looked up to the Führer as a heaven-sent *Übermensch*[6] and desperately sought to ingratiate himself with him.

Hans Frank was one of three children in a middle-class German family. His father was a lawyer. His parents' marriage was unhappy, however, and his mother left while the children were still young to join her lover. Hans Frank was shuttled between both parents. He studied law at university in Munich and quickly radicalized, becoming obsessed by the idea of German superiority in culture and power. In 1923, he joined the Storm Detachment, the paramilitary wing of the Nazi Party. Hitler was as yet only the failed revolutionary of the Beer Hall Putsch, but Frank was quickly seduced by his persona as the great orator of the people.

During his studies, Frank met Brigitte Herbst. At twenty-nine, she was five years older than Frank and employed as a secretary for the Bavarian Parliament. They married on April 2, 1925, in Munich. A year later, with his law degree in hand, he became the first line of defense of Hitler and the Nazi Party during its rise to power.

In 1933, Frank was named Minister of Justice for Bavaria, President of the Academy of German Law, and a Reich Minister without portfolio. He was instrumental in shaping German law to accommodate Hitler's totalitarianism, a fact he would deny. Frank defended his actions, "Constitutional Law in the Third Reich is the legal formulation of the historic will of the Führer, but the historic will of the Führer is not the fulfillment of legal preconditions for his activity."[7] While taking measures to eliminate Jews from the General Government territory of occupied Poland, he declared that in the absence of justice "the state too loses its moral backbone, it sinks into the abyss of night and horror. You can depend on it that I would rather die than give up this idea of justice."[8] He thought of himself as a faithful servant of the law, even a martyr to its cause. Hitler, on the other hand, held the law in utter contempt. For him, lawyers were just a form of common criminal and anyone involved in the practice of law was fundamentally evil or would become so over time.[9]

In late 1939, when Niklas was seven years old, Hans Frank was named governor-general of Occupied Poland, a vast swath of central Poland under Nazi control, and was responsible for overseeing the Jewish ghettos, including the largest in Warsaw, which was created in 1940 and destroyed in 1943. Under his administration, nearly two million Jews were gassed in the extermination camps at Belzec, Sobibor, and Treblinka.[10]

Hans Frank had five children: three boys and two girls. Norman, the eldest son, was born on June 3, 1928, and Niklas, the youngest, on March 9, 1939. Brigitte Frank liked to remind her husband that she had borne him five children. This was an important fact. When she wasn't sure of the identity of the child she was carrying—she was not a model of marital fidelity—she simply aborted, explaining to a suspicious Hans that she miscarried or that the child was too premature to survive.

In the speech he delivered on November 25, 1939, in the Polish city of Radom, Hans Frank outlined his mission as governor-general. "What a pleasure it is to finally tan the hide of the Jewish race. The more of them die, the better."[11] Sixty-six thousand Jews were living in Kraków. Hans Frank's plan was to eradicate them from the city and to build German neighborhoods in the place of the Jewish ones, where one could breathe "good pure German air."[12] Niklas remembered his father telling his mother triumphantly when he was named governor-general, "Brigitte, you'll be the queen of Poland!" Hans Frank's most pressing goal in late 1941 was to solve the problem of what to do with the Jews. He began by executing any Jew found outside the ghetto, which officially launched a manhunt that led to terrible massacres throughout the occupied territory. Jews were no longer sent to the ghettos, either, but transported directly to extermination camps where they were gassed as soon as they arrived.

Years later, Niklas could not remember exactly when it happened but at some point, the three youngest children began to spend most of the year in the family's home in Bavaria with their governess Hilde and only a few months in Kraków. Brigitte did not like to travel with young children.[13] Beginning in 1941, only the two oldest, Norman and Sigrid, lived year-round in Kraków, where they attended the German school.

The Franks were cold, distant parents. Niklas was nicknamed

Fremde (stranger). Once, his father chased him around the dining room table, calling after him, "Who are you, little stranger? You're not even part of this family, are you? What do you want from us, little stranger?" The only thing Niklas ever wanted was to be held by his father, just once. But his presence had a strange effect on people. He liked, he said, to stay quiet and observe his family of criminals.[14]

His mother was a bad-tempered, authoritarian woman. She is the "German mother" whom Niklas describes with such hatred in the book he would write years later.[15] The Frank children have no memories of being cuddled or hugged—or even of their parents' presence. Their parents were, they have said, too busy living their respective lives, leaving the children to be raised by governesses. In his earliest memories, Norman can only see his mother; she spent very little time with him, but his father even less. The Franks entertained regularly, the castle filling with high-ranking Nazi officials, musicians, movie actors, and opera singers. Hans Frank liked to flatter himself that he was a man of culture. In *Kaputt*, the Italian author Curzio Malaparte, who was a war correspondent covering the Eastern Front, portrays Frank as a self-styled Renaissance signore, hosting grandiose dinners of obscene opulence in the midst of his court, while the Polish people were dying of starvation and fear. The despotic Frank was a great admirer of classical music and liked to play Chopin for his guests on his Pleyel piano, never mind that Chopin had been banned by the Nazis; they even destroyed his statue in Warsaw. Malaparte noted, "What makes these executioners suffer is a mystery. They fear nothing more than the weak, the unarmed, the oppressed, the sick: they fear the elderly, women and children, they fear the Jews."[16] The family spent weekends and holidays at the magnificent

Kressendorf palace, outside Kraków. The boys loved the property, where they would shoot birds with their air rifles for hours on end. Norman once killed ninety-eight sparrows.[17]

After Norman rejoined the family in Poland in 1940, Hans Frank would occasionally allow his eldest and favorite son to accompany him on Reich business. Norman claimed he remembered little from this period; he was thirteen at the time. Traveling to Vienna, they would pass near Auschwitz, but Norman said he never knew what was happening there. The Nazis' largest concentration camp was not technically in Frank's jurisdiction, as it lay outside the German zone of occupation, but it was only forty miles from Kraków. Norman knew undoubtedly that it was a camp for Nazi prisoners, but he always insisted he never learned it was an extermination camp until after the war. Niklas does not believe him.[18]

One memory that has stayed with Niklas involves his governess, Hilde. One day, she decided on her own initiative to take Niklas and one of his brothers inside a work camp; it was most likely Plaszow, on the outskirts of Kraków. There, he witnessed a scene that, at the time, he found hilarious: the guards had hoisted some weak, emaciated men onto the backs of donkeys, who kicked and bucked wildly, throwing their riders to the ground, much to the delight of the assembled crowd. Then a nice officer, whom Niklas supposed was a friend of Hilde's, gave him a hot chocolate.[19]

Unlike his oldest brother, the youngest of the Frank children wanted to know everything. His hunger for the truth is his life's work. The only sentiment he feels for his father is loathing. That said, he considers him a "sorry bastard! All he cared about was jewels, castles, handsome uniforms. Human life was worth nothing to him."[20] His was a reign of terror.

Hans Frank boasted, "I am the German king of Poland!" But if anyone observed that a real king never has to say he is one, he would answer: "I have the power of life and death over the Polish people, but I am not the king of Poland. I treat the Poles with the magnanimity and benevolence of a king, but I am not their king. The Polish people are not worthy of a king like me. They are an ungrateful people. . . . They do not deserve the honor of having a German master."[21]

The Franks' marriage was unhappy. Hans was frequently absent. He confided to the psychologist at Nuremberg, Gustave Gilbert, that his wife was too old for him, making them incompatible both physically and emotionally. Brigitte was a far cry from the Nazis' feminine ideal of a devoted mother and housewife. Frau Frank was ambitious, unscrupulous, and the mistress of one of her husband's friends. She was an unfaithful spouse even during their honeymoon when she carried on an affair with a Hamburg shipowner. Yet, after Frank rekindled his relationship with his childhood love, a certain Lilly Groh, Brigitte forced him to come back home. Frank was too valuable a husband to let him leave her, and she would stop at nothing to keep him; she even went to Heinrich Himmler to expose Groh as a Jew. This was enough to convince Niklas that his mother was perfectly aware of the fate of the Jews under the Nazis.[22] She also implored Hitler to stop Frank from divorcing her, saying she "would rather be the widow of a Reich minister than his divorcée." Niklas admits he adores this expression of his mother's.[23] Hans Frank responded by exposing Brigitte's infidelities, notably with his friend, the Doctor Karl Lasch, who was the governor of the Radom district of Nazi occupied Poland. He even went so far as to accuse the lovers of smuggling contraband and he claimed that Lasch was

Niklas's biological father. The question of Niklas's parentage is quickly dismissed in the book Niklas wrote, *Der Vater: Eine Abrechnung (My Father: A Reckoning)*.[24] As an adult, Niklas went to see his father's former secretary, who assured him that his father was not Lasch. All of Hans Frank's sons remembered that their father was frightened of their mother, even when he was imprisoned at Nuremberg.[25]

Beginning in 1942, Hans Frank saw his power considerably undermined. He was criticized for the content of some of the speeches he delivered at German universities, where he argued for an independent justice system. However, it was primarily his corruption and personal enrichment that led to his change of fortunes. Martin Bormann and Heinrich Himmler were openly hostile to him as they worked to expose his incompetence and demanded his dismissal. He was forced to cede to Himmler certain essential powers he held over the police,[26] but, and despite the fact he submitted his resignation to Hitler fourteen times, he remained in his post in Kraków until the total collapse of his authority" in August 1944. On January 17, 1945, he was forced to flee Wawel Castle for Bavaria, following his family who had left several months earlier. Before leaving his stronghold, he took care to arrange for the transfer to Bavaria of his most prized possessions as well as the artworks he had massively pillaged, including paintings by Rembrandt, Raphael, and Leonardo de Vinci's *Lady with an Ermine*. He celebrated his departure with great pomp.[27]

The Frank family moved back to *Schoberhof*, the family's country house, since refurbished, near Schliersee Lake. Hans Frank had purchased it in 1936: a fifty-four-thousand-square-foot structure built in typically Bavarian style with a slate roof, an upper exterior in dark wood, and a white concrete base.

Some of the Frank children spent their childhood years at Schoberhof as veritable apprentice farmers.[28]

It was there that Frank was arrested by American forces on May 4, 1945. Several days earlier, he had entrusted Brigitte with fifty thousand reichsmarks. "My father handed her the money as if she were a prostitute," Niklas would later remember, "in full view of my brother Norman, without an ounce of affection."[29]

Norman had no doubt the Allies were coming for his father. He had been listening to enemy radio and knew they were fast approaching. Hans Frank knew it, too, but he placidly awaited his arrest. One day when Norman visited him in his office at Schoberhof, Frank laid a table with cake and coffee for his oldest and favorite son. "I must be the only minister who is looking forward to his own arrest quite so cheerfully," he confided to Norman.[30] Frank believed he would be exonerated on the evidence of his speeches and private diaries: forty volumes containing a record of his daily activities, from 1939 to 1945, and which he voluntarily turned over to the Allies. He never imagined they would become key elements in his prosecution, but they did, thanks to statements such as the following:

"I must ask you to steel yourselves against all considerations of compassion. We must destroy the Jews wherever we find them, and wherever it is at all possible, in order to maintain the whole structure of the Reich. . . . The Jews are also exceptionally harmful feeders for us. In the Government General we have approximately 2.5 million [Jews], and now perhaps 3.5 million together with persons who have Jewish kin, and so on. We cannot shoot these 3.5 million Jews, we cannot poison them, but we will have to take measures that will lead somehow to successful destruction; and this in connection with the large-scale procedures which are to be discussed in the Reich. The Government General must become as free of Jews as the Reich."[31] Frank was also counting on his conflicts with the Nazi hierarchy to exonerate him of any crime. Norman considered this to be an incomprehensible miscalculation on his father's part. At the moment of his arrest, the American army lieutenant who oversaw the mission, Walter Stein, told the Frank children that their father would be home soon.[32] Niklas was six years old.

Frank made two suicide attempts. On the day of his arrest, he tried to slit his throat after having been beaten by the Allies. He made a second attempt two days later. During his imprisonment at Nuremberg, Frank called Hitler a psychopath and a satanic devil, surrounded by other diabolical "men of action" like Bormann and Himmler, and he tried to convince the Allies that all of the atrocities committed by the Third Reich had been secretly planned by those three officials.[33] Hans Frank was among those many Nazis who were unable to admit their guilt; it was the devil Hitler who made him do it.

Back at Schoberhof, Brigitte Frank had her hands full trying to protect the family's property. The house was looted at night by Polish and Ukrainian prisoners who had been freed from the work camps, but Brigitte had managed to hide a box of jewels with her neighbor. Niklas would recall that she later bartered some of these for food at a camp for displaced Jews.[34]

On another occasion, a heavily armed American soldier attempted to help himself to the contents of the wine cellar and lined Brigitte and the children against a wall as if to shoot them. Niklas remembered that his mother calmly asked him to spare the children, before the soldier's superior officer ended the charade.

The family was forced to leave in August 1945, with only two suitcases and some furs, seeking lodgings in an inn before finding a small two-room apartment in the neighboring village of Neuhaus am Schliersee. Once the furs had been sold, Brigitte sent the children out to beg for food. She tried to enroll Norman in the only nearby school for his age but the principal refused to admit the son of a war criminal. By this time, Norman was eighteen. With no other choice than to continue his schooling at home, he failed his exams and never went on to university.

Five months passed without any news of Hans, until the family learned that he had tried to commit suicide again. They had been following the trial on the radio. In September 1946, the entire family went to see him for the last time, before the verdict was delivered. Norman found his father thin and greatly changed. Hans delivered a last word of advice to his eldest son, remembered later by Norman: "He told me to be strong and always remember never to speak my mind unless I first thought carefully about what I would say."[35]

The memory of this last meeting still fills Niklas with rage: "I remember it very clearly. I was sitting on my mother's knees and he was sitting behind a window [. . .] and he was friendly and laughing. It was my strongest impression of him because it was the last time I saw him. And I knew it was the last time. And he said to me, 'Ah, Niki, in three months' time we will have a wonderful Christmas Eve in our house.' And I sat there thinking, 'He is lying.' He knew he was going to be executed. Why was he lying to me?"[36]

To this day, Niklas cannot understand why his father never spoke plainly to him or left him with a word of advice, saying: "I am going to die, and I am guilty, and you will never meet me again, but here is something for your later life."[37] Niklas was seven years old when his father was sentenced; the news was everywhere in the small village where they were living, and a topic of conversation at school, as well. He never cried over his father's death.[38] Yet his father's lack of remorse still weighs unbearably on him. "We inherited his faults," he has said,[39] and he struggles to find words sufficiently strong to describe his father, this "weak," "vain," "hypocritical," "cowardly," "murderer" and "ass-kisser." But he admits, "It was this coward who built the gas chambers."[40]

Found guilty of war crimes and crimes against humanity at Nuremberg, Hans Frank was executed by hanging on October 16, 1946. Several months after his arrest, he had converted to Catholicism under the guidance of an Irish Franciscan father, Sixtus O'Connor. Niklas believes that if anyone could have learned anything about his father, it was Pater Sixtus. This new Frank declared: "It is as though I am two people—me, myself, Frank here—and the other Frank, the Nazi leader. And sometimes I wonder how that man Frank could have done those things."[41] But Niklas also thinks the priest disliked his father. When he asked O'Connor what his father's last words were as he walked to the gallows, O'Connor told him he did not remember. He sent the Frank children their father's book of prayers after his death.[42]

Norman believed a death sentence was preferable to a life sentence, such as Rudolf Hess received, reasoning that it would have been very difficult to bear such a long sentence. "A life sentence for my father would have been a life sentence for the whole family."[43]

Frank was executed with ten other Nazi officials (twelve were sentenced to death, but Göring had already committed suicide and Martin Bormann was convicted in absentia). However, he was the only one of the ten to go smiling to his death. He had the look of a man who had been freed of his demons. Standing on the gallows, he had this to say: "I am grateful to you for my treatment during my detention and I ask God in His mercy to take me to Him."[44] A palm reader had told him in 1935 that he would be the center of a large trial and would die a violent death before he was fifty. Given that he was a lawyer, Frank was not surprised by her prediction.[45] He was forty-six when he was hanged.

Brigitte Frank met the same fate as all of the other wives of Nazi officials who were condemned at Nuremberg: she was arrested under orders of the minister of denazification, Alfred Loritz, in May 1947. She was in the kitchen of the apartment in Neuhaus, in Upper Bavaria, when the police came to arrest her. She became distraught when she had to leave four children behind her with nothing and no means of support. Her eldest daughter, Sigrid, had been married since 1945. It was the first time Niklas ever saw his mother cry; he and his siblings had only known her to be a hard woman. When the verdicts were delivered at Nuremberg, she kept a list of the names of the accused and drew a cross next to the name of each condemned man or, in the case of a different sentence, wrote that next to the name of the accused. She coolly drew a cross next to her husband's name and did not shed a tear at his execution.

Brigitte Frank was taken to Göggingen, near Augsburg, to join the ranks of Emmy Göring, Ilse Hess, Luise Funck, who was the wife of the former Reich Minister of the Economy, and

Henriette von Schirach, the wife of Baldur von Schirach, who was the head of the Hitler Youth. Brigitte Frank was prisoner number 1467. These women who had lived in great luxury during the war learned to make do with straw mattresses, rats, and bugs in prison. Hunger and close quarters became their daily reality. Their children were allowed to visit only occasionally, and the women worried constantly for their safety and health in devastated, postwar Germany.

They also had some astonishing conversations. Brigitte Frank congratulated Emmy Göring for the "magnificent" death of her husband, thanks to the cyanide pill he kept on him, unlike Hans Frank. Emmy Göring did not miss an opportunity to taunt Brigitte. "So now the Queen of Poland has lost the Reich and her husband both!"[46] Sometimes the women raised a toast to "the health of their dead men" and to Adolf Hitler "who took their husbands' best years." Brigitte Frank denied the denazification court's accusation that she ever purchased jewelry on the black market or by any other means. But when she was faced with incontrovertible evidence and could find no other argument in her defense, she declared, "I am not an anti-Semite."[47] On the several occasions when her son visited her in prison, she brought him to listen to Ilse Koch, the wife of Buchenwald's lead commandant, who liked to sing old Nazi songs. Ilse Koch was known as "the Bitch" or "the Witch" because of her sadism. Her songs made Brigitte laugh.

She sported a tan when she was released in mid-September 1947.[48] She told her children: "It was my best vacation ever. Emmy Göring liked it very much too."[49] The two women had grown close during their detention. Brigitte was impressed by the list of jewels Emmy owned, as enumerated by the denazification court.[50]

In 1951, Norman made the decision to leave the family and emigrate to Argentina. His presence was discovered, however, by Argentine Nazis, who looked to him to take up his father's causes. He sought to hide himself by working in a mine near the Bolivian border.

That same year, Niklas was sent to a boarding school in Wyk auf Föhr, where he stayed until 1959, when he turned twenty. He looks back on those years as an incredibly happy period of his life. Far from home, he no longer had to listen to his mother's shouting. The school observed the extremely strict rules of the Teutonic Order. Niklas felt right at home. Mornings were reserved for classes; afternoons for sports. The other students knew who Niklas's father was, but showed little interest. Niklas found a father figure in the school's Pastor Lohmann, who had made it his mission to open his doors to the children of the Nazi Party, showing them it was possible for people who were not like them to love them.[51] One day, when he was twelve, Niklas wrote at the top of a letter he was composing to his mother "Niklas Frank, Prince of Poland." Lohmann gave him a stern warning: "You must never do that again."[52] Also at the school were Adolf and Barthold Ribbentrop, the sons of Joachim von Ribbentrop, the Reich's Foreign Minister. They never kept company with Niklas, however, who does not remember that they ever discussed their fathers.

Brigitte Frank was at that time living on a monthly pension of just five hundred marks, of the five thousand she was promised from the government when it seized her property in 1947.[53]

In 1953, she willingly sold the memoirs Hans Frank had penned shortly before his death, published under the title *Im Angesicht des Galgens* (*The View From the Gallows*). It was a bestseller in Germany, where it was sold and read—in secret—by the thousands. As the book's editor, Brigitte Frank made herself a tidy sum of around 200,000 deutschmarks.

In his memoirs, Hans Frank discusses the question of Hitler's Jewish ancestry. Under the influence of his nephew, William Patrick Hitler, who was the son of his half brother, Alois, Hitler asked him in the late 1930s to research the records of Maria Schicklgruber, his paternal grandmother. She had been employed as a cook by a Jew named Leopold Frankenberger before giving birth to Adolf's father, Alois Hitler. Hans Frank wrote in his memoirs that he had found letters exchanged by Maria and the Frankenberger family regarding a request for child support. Adolf Hitler interpreted the letters, not as proof that the Frankenberger's son was his grandfather, but that his grandmother Maria had managed to blackmail the family for money by threatening to reveal the paternity of this illegitimate son. Respected historians such as Ian Kershaw have dismissed Frank's revelations, but others have investigated further. As far as Niklas is concerned, his father found no conclusive proof of Hitler's alleged Jewish ancestry, but he enjoys the story for demonstrating that the man who used the question of ancestry to decide the fates of millions of people had very uncertain origins himself.

When the book stopped selling, around 1958, Brigitte began to rent beds in her house to travelers arriving at the train station in Munich: five marks for the night. By hanging sheets between mattresses lined up in her living room, she could sleep up to five people at a time.

Niklas adored the theater but after his graduation, he decided to pursue studies in law, history, sociology, and German literature.

He never earned a diploma but he became a journalist and a writer. He was the Culture editor at both the erotic magazine *Her* and then at *Playboy* where he worked for three years. He also worked for the German magazine *Stern* for twenty years. Unlike some children of Nazi officials, Niklas has been perfectly clear: "I am not afraid of the past; I want to know everything."[54] To this day, he carries with him a photo of his father, taken just after his death. When asked why, he answers, "I am pleased by what the picture shows: he is dead."[55]

When a parent feels no regret or guilt for crimes he has committed, it can have very different effects on his children; they might choose to follow their father's lead and feel no guilt, or they might feel so troubled by what their father did that they reject him completely. Niklas Frank falls into this category: it is intolerable to him that his father never expressed remorse or regret and that he tried to justify his actions. "No, he never regretted anything . . . I hate him, that bastard who's burning in hell and who hounds me," he says about his father.

> "Not a day goes by that I don't have the horrible impression he's manipulating me like a puppet on a string. . . . Does that sound unbelievable? Even as a child, I always felt like I was living in a family of criminals. It was a vague feeling, but I was convinced of it, unlike my older brothers and sisters who always refused to face the facts. It wasn't long before I saw photos of the camps on the front pages of the newspapers: piles of naked bodies, skeletons in rags, and, you know, children holding out their tiny wrists to show their number. . . . They were the same age as me, they were being held so close to the castle in Poland where my father was stockpiling his gold and where I was acting like a prince in my pedal car. It

was a horrifying realization . . . I tried like crazy to imagine myself in those photos; I tried to feel their suffering in my own body, the anguish of those Jews who were going to die. I tried to be them. They still haunt me."[56]

His father's death also torments him. He imagines his father's final moments: the wait, the corridor, the priest, the thirteen steps leading up to the gallows, and then finally the noose and death. Niklas tried to understand his father; he pored over every document he could lay his hands on before finally coming to a conclusion: "I could find nothing to explain what he did, except greed and fanatical ambition. And despite the atrocious things he said about the Jews, I think he didn't give a damn and was not truly anti-Semitic. If Hitler had decided to do the same thing to the French or the Chinese, he would have delivered the same impassioned speeches using Nietzsche, Schiller, Goethe, and Corneille."[57]

In an interview he granted to the German magazine *Der Spiegel*, Niklas admitted he would have liked to have a baker for a father. But like other children of Nazi leaders, he thought it would have been even worse for him if he had been the son of Himmler or Göring.[58]

Niklas believes his father "deserved to be executed and was delighted to be."[59] He also questions his father's late conversion to Catholicism, believing he only did so for absolution. However, he recognizes he shares some of his father's traits; he considers himself to be a brilliant liar and an excellent speaker with an aggressive sense of humor—his father's sense of humor.[60] The book he published in Germany in 1997 about his father was virulently criticized, especially by some other Nazi children: Klaus von Schirach and Martin Adolf Bormann, in particular. The latter was a professor of theology at the time and expressed regret he and Niklas had never spoken about their fathers. For some of these children, rejecting or cursing their fathers was out of the question. For others, the book was too violent, in both its scenes and its language.

Niklas's brother, Michael, attacked him publicly in an open letter to *Stern*, which he ended as follows: "My brother Niki is and will always be a stranger."[61] Even his closest friends broke with him. The book was shocking right from its opening scene involving masturbation.

Niklas wrote, "The child I was appropriated your death. The nights leading up to October 16 became sacred to me. I would lie down naked on the sour-smelling linoleum in the water closet, my legs sticking straight out, my left hand holding my flaccid penis and then, lightly rubbing it, I could start to see you."[62] At the time of those events, Niklas was living with his four brothers and sisters in a small apartment in Neuhuas, at Dürnbachstrasse 7.

A journalist once explained to Niklas that his orgasm was the sign of his desire to outlive his father; Niklas has said that interpretation was an eye-opener for him.[63] His own understanding of the situation is more complex, however, and he openly criticizes the German people: "A day doesn't go by that I don't think about my father and everything the Germans did. The world will never forget. Wherever I go abroad, as soon as I say I am German, people think immediately of Auschwitz. I think they are perfectly right to."[64]

Later, *Stern* serialized a fifth of his book under the title, "My Father, the Nazi Murderer." The weekly series ran for seven weeks. There, Niklas recounts how, on the anniversary of his father's death, he masturbates under his father's portrait or imagines himself dissecting him.

His mother is also raked over the coals: a provincial upstart driven by social status. "My mother was as cynical as she was cowardly. She was mad about furs and would have herself driven in a Mercedes, accompanied by an SS guard, to buy on the cheap those corsets the Jews made so well. She didn't give a damn that they were starving."[65]

In Konrad Adenauer's postwar Germany, whose slogan was "Don't ask questions! Rebuild the country!" Niklas regretted he never asked his mother to answer for what she did during the war. About those years, Niklas had this to say: "Don't believe for a minute that nostalgia for the Reich just disappeared! Every measure was taken to prevent the regime from facing trial, to stop sons from questioning their fathers, to block any kind of sincere introspection. We'll pay for it! Thankfully, media from around the world are watching us closely and are up in arms as soon as a Turk is attacked or a Jewish cemetery is vandalized. Without that, everything could happen all over. I love the German people but I haven't a shred of confidence in them."[66]

For Niklas, his mother was a fundamentally immoral woman who, like many Germans, consciously profited from the Third Reich. In the book he published about her in 2005, *Meine deutsche Mutter* (*My German Mother*), he lets loose his hatred for this woman who never showed any remorse. At least, he writes, she never tried to glorify her husband and never again spoke of the Reich, except for a single anecdote about Hitler's gallantry that she delighted in retelling. She was wholly absorbed by the task of satisfying her children's needs and had no time for anything else.[67]

Niklas tried to kill her with an overdose of her medicine in 1959. She had suffered a heart attack and had been hospitalized at the University of Munich hospital, where Niklas came to see her to celebrate his twentieth birthday a few days early. She was overweight, and her legs were swollen by water retention but she wanted to look nice for her son and had asked a nurse to do her makeup for the occasion. Her heavily powdered and rouged face, with bright red lipstick, looked garish to Niklas. She knew Niklas had never loved her but she couldn't refrain from asking him point-blank: "Tell me, you never loved me, my child?" He didn't answer, and she filled in the silence—as if nothing had just happened—by instructing him to follow his father's example and study law, wishing him "an important future."[68] Brigitte Frank died a few days later on March 9, Niklas's birthday. She was sixty-three.[69]

Norman spent three years in Argentina, a period he described as a "release" from Germany and his family. His mother "took all his air." He also spoke openly of his father's affair with his childhood love and has said that he could understand why he wanted to leave his wife for her.[70] After he returned to Munich, Norman lived in his mother's apartment, with portraits of both of his parents and some of the family furniture. Niklas's older brother was tormented by the past and admired the courage of his youngest sibling when he wrote about their father and attacked him so virulently with words that were as crude as his gestures. Norman found it more difficult to question his father. He loved him and was never able to detach himself completely from him; as the oldest son, he saw firsthand his father's rise through the ranks of the Nazi regime, an experience that Niklas believes prevented Norman from making a successful life for himself, both personally and professionally.

Niklas has a daughter but Norman refused to have children for fear of passing on his father's genes. His one love, Ellens, was married, and Norman paid her husband ten thousand deutschmarks to divorce her. She committed suicide on her fortieth birthday, June 3, 1967. Niklas thinks Norman married an ardent anti-Semite in his second marriage.[71]

Right up until his death, Norman kept a painted portrait of his father over his bed in the Munich apartment, even though he had long abused alcohol to try to forget him. In *Bruder Norman!*, the last book in his family trilogy, Niklas discusses his brother's addiction, which ruined his life. The book opens on Norman's death, and its subtitle is Norman's mantra: "My father was a Nazi criminal but I loved him." Norman, who, in his last years, rarely left the armchair that was placed in front of the window of his apartment, reached out to Niklas at the end of his life, and the book was born of a conversation they had about their lives, or more precisely, their father's. Their mother's repugnant morals, their parents' near divorce, Hitler, Hans Frank's execution and conversion to Catholicism are all discussed. The two brothers hold radically different views on these subjects, however: Niklas wanted to understand everything that Norman wanted to forget. Norman's tombstone is inscribed with this epitaph: "Now you are free from the torments of your love for your father" (*Jetzt bist du all die Liebesqualen durch deinen Vater los*).

Norman, whom Hans Frank nicknamed "Normi," did not share Niklas's interpretation of the family's years in Poland. He was an adolescent at the time and perfectly able to understand the world around him, but he claimed that he was too preoccupied by puberty to notice. To get to the German school in Kraków on his bicycle, he crossed the city but he said he never noticed the SS barracks next to it. He didn't remember "the Jews, half-naked in the cold, unloading coal from a truck," but one of his classmates did, in perfect detail.[72]

His younger brothers and sisters were not often in Kraków, and his sister, Sigrid, had her own life. His only memories of those years were of his distant parents and his solitude, nothing else. "The time of the General Government was strange. Overall, I was happy. I was going through puberty and that was more interesting to me than anything happening around me."[73] After the war, when he read his father's writings, he felt ashamed. "It was not the father I loved. It's such a contradiction in him, I can't understand it. How could he be so cultured and good to me and then say things so stupid and hateful?"[74]

Unlike Niklas, Norman never wanted to believe his father had played a role in the extermination of millions of Jews, although he remembered seeing trucks rumble through the neighborhood with AUSCHWITZ written in large letters on their sides. It was not until he was seventy-seven that he could face the truth, as related in the last volume of the Frank trilogy. Niklas credits him, however, as the only one of the Frank children who ever confronted their father; one day, he was playing soccer with other German children below the castle, when they heard shots and saw a group of men lined up against the castle walls fall to the ground in a pool of blood. He was fourteen or fifteen at the time and he asked his father why those men, who had been singing the Polish national anthem a moment earlier, had just been executed. "I don't want to hear another word about this until after the war,"[75] his father told him.

The two brothers had different feelings as well about

carrying the Frank name; for Norman, it was a handicap, but Niklas felt people treated him with greater respect. They both agreed, however, that it played a determining role in their lives.[76]

Of the five Frank children, only Norman and Niklas admitted their father was a criminal. The other three lived different, often tragic, lives but refused to accept the truth. The oldest daughter, Sigrid, emigrated with her husband to South Africa in 1966 and was a supporter of the Apartheid regime. Niklas recalled in an interview that Sigrid was also a negationist, telling Niklas during a phone conversation: "If six million Jews had been burned, everybody would have burned [in] just six seconds, which just proves that it's all lies."[77]

The Franks' second daughter, Brigitte, developed cancer and committed suicide in 1981 at the age of forty-six, the same age as her father when he died. Niklas has said that she was convinced her father was innocent and she could never bear living without him.[78] She was the mother of two children, the oldest of whom, then eight years old, was sleeping with her when she swallowed a fatal dose of sleeping pills.[79]

The third of the Frank boys, Michael, died, obese, at the age of fifty-three. He drank thirteen liters of milk every day.

Niklas is the only surviving Frank child. He continues the tireless search for the truth that he began over fifty years ago. He is his father's principal biographer, despite the hatred he feels for him. He is outraged by the position adopted by other Nazi children, such as Martin Adolf Bormann, of whom he has said: "Patricide is a taboo as old as the dawn of time, and Bormann's son has acted no differently. An incredible number of German schools invited him to speak because he told everyone that his father was not only a criminal but a loving father too.

It's a fairly revolting strategy, adopted to diminish his father's guilt, and eighty million hypocritical Germans were happy to fall in line with him."[80]

Niklas lives with his wife in the countryside north of Hamburg. He gives talks in schools several times a year. Asked about the current migrant crisis in Europe, and Germany's policy toward immigrants in 2015, he calls it a wonderful response but thinks that the overwhelming majority of Germans are silently opposed to it.

Martin Adolf Bormann Jr.

The "Crown Prince"

On April 25, 1971, in a late afternoon rainstorm, the driver of a white Opel lost control of his car and crashed head-on into an American military vehicle. The camouflage green truck was driving without its lights on when the Opel tried to turn onto the same highway. The impact was so strong that the body of the car crumpled like an accordion, completely destroying the front of the vehicle and trapping its driver—now barely alive—inside. A few meters away, a car mechanic saw the truck pass and heard the crash shortly after. He rushes to the scene: is the driver alive or dead? The two American soldiers look on while the mechanic struggles to get to the driver, trapped between crushed metal and the dashboard. Using a crowbar, he manages to pry away the car's frame, piece by piece. As he gets closer to the driver, he can see his face. He looks familiar. He knows this man. He has certainly seen him before, but where? Is he someone from the mechanic's past? From that time he prefers to forget and never speak of? That was when he was a driver. Could it be that he drove this man, but when? The driver looks to be about forty years old, in which case he would have been a child all those years ago.

After wrestling with a final piece of twisted metal, he is able to pull the man free and begins resuscitation measures, still trying to place this face from his past. Finally, he can see him, a boy of about eleven, sitting quietly on the back seat of a black sedan. He is with his mother and his two sisters. He is dressed in lederhosen with suspenders, a red checked shirt and woolen knee-socks: the traditional clothing of Upper Bavaria, where his former boss owned a house. That was when the mechanic was employed as a driver by Heinrich Himmler, the chief of the SS and the German police. But the seriously injured man whom he is holding now in his arms is none other than the son of Martin Bormann, the Führer's personal secretary. Decades have passed but now the memories all come flooding back. He often drove the child back and forth between Gmund and Obersalzberg, where the Führer had a mountain retreat. Something now makes him look closer at the man: despite the blood that is everywhere, he can see that the man is wearing what looks like a cassock. The Bormann boy, a priest?

A first-response team arrives and the memory fades. The accident victim disappears behind the doors of the ambulance that will take him to the closest hospital. His condition is critical; his injuries are life-threatening. No one can say if he will survive. He slips into a coma. Ten days will pass before he awakes.

The oldest of the ten children of Martin Bormann and his wife, Gerda, Martin Adolf Jr., was born April 14, 1930, in

Grünwald. His parents named him after the Führer, and he was Hitler's first godson. His godmother was Ilse Hess, the wife of the Deputy Führer, Rudolf Hess, whom Martin Bormann served as his chief of staff. Later, following the customs of the Nazis, the Bormann's would no longer have their children baptized.

Martin Bormann became known as the "Brown Eminence" as he assumed ever greater power and responsibility. He was also relentlessly calculating, earning him the nickname "Machiavelli of the office desk."[1] He was born in 1900 into the petty bourgeoisie of Saxony Anhalt. He first made a name for himself as a convicted accomplice to murder in 1923, before falling under the spell of a certain Adolf Hitler. He was short, stocky, and unattractive but he became so indispensable that, some said, his power surpassed Hitler's. He began his career in the office of Rudolf Hess, the Nazi Party's secretary, and gradually moved up the ranks to finally supplant his boss. He controlled all communication with the Führer, who trusted him completely and designated him as the executor of his will shortly before he died. Bormann was convinced that the Reich could win the war, right up until its defeat. Unlike other Nazi officials, he never attempted to negotiate a peace treaty with the Allies, even when the end was near.

His career took a decisive turn when Rudolf Hess left on his mad peace mission to Great Britain on May 10, 1941, following which he was named Hess's successor as the Head of the *Parteikanzlei*, or the Chancellery of the National Socialist Party. His rise was unstoppable. In April 1943, he was officially appointed Personal Secretary to the Führer. It was also Bormann who, for Hitler's fiftieth birthday in 1939, made him a present of the Eagle's Nest that would become his mountain retreat: a chalet perched on a rocky outcrop at the summit of the Kehlstein, at an altitude of six thousand feet. He became the man in charge at Obersalzberg. Nothing escaped Bormann's reach, and Hitler praised his abilities. He was feared by all, including other officials, even the likes of Heinrich Himmler, Hermann Göring, and Rudolf Hess. Albert Speer called him the most dangerous man in Hitler's circle. Bormann held a unique power over him. Beginning in early 1935, Bormann was given control of Hitler's personal finances, which he managed magisterially. Hitler's income included royalties collected from *Mein Kampf* and the use of the Führer's image on postage stamps and from the sale of plots of land in Obersalzberg.

Speer was not the only one who was wary of Bormann; all of Hitler's inner circle hated and feared him. Everyone who suffered a fall from grace detected a plot hatched against him by Bormann. His power reached its apogee during the years of the Reich's decline. His proximity to the Führer allowed him to progressively eclipse even the highest-ranking Nazi officials.

His wife, Gerda Buch, was the daughter of another important figure in the National Socialist Party and a close friend of Hitler's. Gerda and Martin were married in a Nazi ceremony on September 2, 1929, and began a happy marriage. Martin Bormann wrote lengthy correspondence to his wife during his frequent absences. In the summer of 1936, the family moved from Pullach, near Munich, to Obersalzberg. Martin Adolf was born in 1930. His memories of his early, carefree childhood were few, but one memory stood out: one day when he was playing in the garden, his sister was hit in the head by a swing, and Martin, fearing a tanning, hid himself in the cellar—so well, in fact, that no one found him. However, when night fell and plunged him into darkness, he panicked; he was so traumatized by the experience that his mother considered the fright was punishment enough.[2]

In addition to a baby sister who died just after birth, Martin Adolf had nine siblings: twins Ilse and Erengard Franziska (1931), Irmgard (1933), Rudolf Gerhard (1934), Heinrich Hugo (1936), Eva Ute (1938), Gerda (1940), Fred Hartmut (1942), and Volker (1943).

Martin Adolf went to the primary school in Berchtesgaden but his parents, who were openly anti-Christian, insisted he be excused from religious education classes. Martin Adolf remembered that during catechism hour, he was sent to another classroom where he did his homework on a bench at the rear of the room. He realized from a very young age that he was different from other children. He was the only one excluded from catechism class and never understood why. When he asked his parents, they would simply reply, "We don't need it."

He watched as work on the Führer's mountain progressed, according to his father's orders. First, the residents had to be evicted, beginning in the early 1930s. Next, the entire area was cordoned off as a high-security zone and entirely rebuilt to accommodate the Reich's highest-ranking officials and to host VIPs. Obersalzberg is on the German-Austrian border and faces Hitler's favorite peak, the Untersberg, in the Berchtesgaden Alps. The Bormann children were raised in isolation in a house in the secure zone. This Nazi redoubt, which was guarded by the SS, was also the home of such Nazi leaders as Hermann Göring and Albert Speer and their families.

In addition to those children, Martin Adolf had for playmates the children of the gardener, the driver, and the chef at Obersalzberg. They played cops and robbers, cowboys and Indians, and war games, like all children their age. No visitors from the village were allowed, although some tried to get a peek at the "mountain people" who lived at such a great distance from the villagers. The zone measured almost three square miles and was fenced in on all sides. Albert Speer joked that it looked like a "big game hunting preserve" but it was a world unto itself, rigid and conventional, whose inhabitants were out of touch with the world on the other side.

Martin Adolf remembered the visits of dignitaries like Neville Chamberlain, Edouard Daladier, and Benito Mussolini, the prime ministers of Great Britain, France, and Italy respectively, who often visited the Führer for several days at a time. He was always made to dress for these occasions, and he never forgot his handshake with Mussolini; it left such an impression on him, in fact, that everything else about that day faded from his memory.

His mother, Gerda, was one of the rare Nazi wives who corresponded to the Nazis' ideal woman: she was a housewife who could usually be found in her kitchen, she paid no attention to politics, and she took her role as a procreator of Nazi children very seriously. She bore Martin Bormann eleven children and was ever faithful to her adulterous husband. Above all, she demonstrated her commitment to "the cause" by encouraging polygamy to increase the birthrate. She wanted to provide even more children to the Führer and wrote to him enthusiastically: "We should introduce a law at the end of the war like the law passed at the end of the Thirty Years' War, which allowed healthy productive men to have two wives." Martin Bormann wrote in the margins: "Yes, absolutely, for the coming battle that will decide the fate of our nation."[3]

Gerda was always thrilled when her husband was able to seduce some actress or another: the important thing was that he always had at his disposal a woman "of serviceable condition." When he and the actress Manja Behrens started an affair, Gerda congratulated him and expressed her hope that she might bear him a child as quickly as possible. Bormann was not shy about bringing his mistress to Obersalzberg, where she stayed in the family home. His boorishness was hardly appreciated by everyone, but Gerda's consent kept the affair from taking on the dimensions of a scandal.[4] As for Bormann, he could not have been more pleased by his wife's attitude and her opinions on the role of women, especially since he had a huge sexual appetite. Gerda was a fanatical supporter of the Reich until the end. She even wanted the Reich to create a "National Emergency Marriage."[5] On the eve of the Reich's fall, as her husband was beginning to realize the gravity of the situation, she wrote to him, "One day, the Reich of our dreams will emerge. Shall we, I wonder, or our children, live to see it?"[6]

In school, Martin Adolf was not a very diligent student, and he paid for it; his father scolded him severely and packed him off to an Ordensburgen, a Nazi Party academy, to be "trained." Hitler had taken steps to create a system of schools to educate the Nazi elite, but none of the Reich's officials, regardless of how fanatic, availed themselves of it. Bormann was the only one who sent his son there, and only as a punishment. Martin Adolf was ten when he entered the Reich school at Feldafing on Lake Starnberg. It had been created by Ernst Röhm in 1933 as a preparatory school for the Nazi elite. Each regional Gauleiter could propose three candidates, but Munich and Berlin were allowed five each. Martin Adolf was the only student who bypassed that system; essentially, his father pulled strings to have him admitted. He began training to become a paramilitary soldier, but, as Bormann's son, he found it difficult to blend in. The curriculum also proved challenging for him, especially physical education, which was given priority in the curriculum. By force of will, he finally made a place for himself. In his National Socialism class, he had to memorize the party program and study *Mein Kampf.* Later, in the upper grades, the required text was Alfred Rosenberg's *Der Mythus des zwanzigsten Jahrhunderts* (*The Myth of the Twentieth Century*),[7] although neither the students nor the teachers could make sense of it. He would later say that even his father was never able to read it start to finish, despite many attempts.

His time at the Ordensburgen would be a watershed in the life of the young Martin Adolf. He would never live with his family again; his removal was definitive. He would only visit his family during school holidays, when his father was usually away. When he and his father were together, Bormann was extremely severe with his son. Once, when Martin Adolf saluted the Führer with a "Heil Hitler," his father slapped him violently; the custom when addressing Hitler directly was to say, "Heil, mein Führer." Bormann's cruelty had a profound effect on the boy, especially since it was never offset by even the slightest display of affection. There was no communication or human warmth at all between them. On visits, Martin Adolf usually spent his time helping a gardener or working on a farm in Obersalzberg. He only had good memories of the war years, although he was conscious of his strained relations with his father.

Because of his extremely busy schedule accompanying Hitler on all of his official business, Bormann only visited the academy once, in 1943. Martin Adolf recalled clearly that he questioned his father: "What is National Socialism?"

His father's response was brief and direct and confirmed for him beyond a shadow of a doubt that the Nazi movement had no meaningful ideological underpinning but rested instead on unfailing allegiance to its "god," Hitler: "National Socialism," Bormann told him, "is the will of the Führer!"[8]

In his book, *Leben gegen Schatten* (*Live Despite the Darkness*), published in 1996, Martin Adolf explains that the absence of any clear program left National Socialism open to interpretation by the party's factions. Hitler intervened as little as possible, and even then his explanations were ambiguous, which made it easier to play those factions against each other. According to Martin Adolf, it was "the will of Hitler" and the "religious roots" of the Nazi ideology that justified anti-Semitism and the hatred for anything resembling Christianity.[9]

"What do I know, if anything, about my father?" Martin Adolf has asked himself. He grew up without ever knowing the elder Martin Bormann and rarely meeting him; his childhood was dictated by his strictly disciplinarian education founded on the veneration of the Führer, "God's emissary," and played to the soundtrack of Nazi music. He saw his father for the last time during the Christmas holidays in 1943. The school closed on April 23, 1945. Martin Adolf was fifteen. It was understood that the oldest students were to be sent to the front; however, the imminent capitulation of the Reich put an end to that plan.

"The worst was when, at two in the morning on May 1, the radio broadcast the news of the death of the Führer. For me, that was the end. I remember the moment vividly, but I cannot describe the silence that greeted the news ... it must have lasted four hours. No one said a word, but eventually people began to go outside, and almost immediately, there was a gunshot, then another, and another. Inside, no one spoke, there was no sound, only the gunshots outside. We thought we were all going to die. . . . I saw no future for myself. Suddenly, behind the bodies that covered the little courtyard, another boy, who was eighteen, appeared. He invited me to come sit next to him. The air smelled fresh, birds were singing, we were still alive. I know that, if we hadn't been there for each other in that precise moment, neither of us would still be here. I know it."[10]

This was the beginning of a new era for Martin Adolf: the end of the *Ubermensch* and the dawn of the human community of God's children.

The students at the academy fled in all directions to find their families on their own. Martin Adolf, whose nickname was the *Krönzi* ("the Crown Prince"), returned to Obersalzberg in his Hitler Youth uniform with a swastika armband. His mother had already left, however, headed for South Tyrol. She would take up residence in Wolkenstein—where Gudrun Himmler and her mother would also end up—and change her name to Bergmann.

Bormann's secretary was still in his office. He ushered Martin Adolf in, gave him an ordinary gray jacket and told him to burn his uniform immediately and to change his name. He gave him forged identity papers under the name of Bergmann and stamped "KLV-Lager 39, Steinach a. Brenner." With that, the young man presented himself to the National Socialist Party's district chief, the Gauleiter of Salzburg, Gustav Adolf Scheel, who gave him new marching orders: to report to St. Johann's school in Pongau as an apprentice agriculturist. Before he arrived there, however, all the students had been released; Martin Adolf found no one. The following day, walking in the streets, he caught sight of a black Mercedes sedan that looked exactly like his family's car. He even thought he saw his mother, but realized it was just an illusion. He decided to leave and, upon crossing paths with a retreating Nazi convoy, followed it.

He was terrified, convinced that he would be executed on the spot if the Allies captured him, Bormann's son. He had no idea what had happened to his father. He eventually heard rumors that his father had died fleeing the Allies' attack on Berlin.

The Israeli psychologist Dan Bar-On, who interviewed Martin Adolf forty years after the war, reports that the younger Bormann was unable to control his emotions when he spoke of that period.[11] He had no knowledge of the persecution of the Jews, had never heard of Kristallnacht nor ever seen a Star of David, because "there were no Jews in Berchtesgaden or at Obersalzberg." No one discussed these in the Bormann home, either. He was more affected by the persecution of Christians, saying, "[T]he Catholic Church was presented as being an extension, so to speak, of Zionism. The confrontation with the Jews was considered to be over, finished, taken care of more or less."[12]

In late May 1945, his wanderings took him into the mountains. He was sick with severe salmonella poisoning and stopped to rest at an old farmhouse in Hinterthal, south of Salzburg, on the Austrian side of the German border. The farmer living there asked no questions and simply took him in. Martin Adolf said his name was Bergmann and that he was from Munich— he gave a false address—and that both his parents had died in the air strikes; he did not want anyone to try to find them. He had not forgotten the advice his father's secretary had given him: under no circumstances was he to reveal his true identity.

He understood that the name Bormann would be a death sentence in postwar Germany. Some children of Nazi leaders had to confront the complete silence their families maintained about the war, but Martin Adolf Bormann was forced to live the rest of his life in complete anonymity.

The family who took him in cared for him as if he were their own child. They were pious people who understood from the first time they took the boy to church that he had had no religious instruction. As for Martin Adolf, he said he learned from his time with them what Christian living meant: the opposite of everything he had been taught. On this isolated mountain, he discovered a loving family and a new home and found an ideal environment for reflection, even shepherding the family's animals. However, he could not escape the revelations that were coming to light about war crimes and the Holocaust, of which he had never heard speak before. The family's only news outlet was the renowned Austrian daily, *Salzburger Nachrichten*, which opened his eyes to the horrific extent of the Nazis' barbarity.

It was no longer possible to ignore his father's role in the war. Photos taken at Bergen-Belsen would haunt him for the rest of his life. The Ordensburgen had used laborers from Dachau, but Martin Adolf assumed they were criminals. In any case, they looked nothing at all like the walking cadavers the Allies discovered at the camps in 1945. He finally understood the abysmal horror that humans can perpetrate.[13] He also developed a clear reasoning for the feelings of guilt that children can have for the crimes committed by their parents:

The Fourth Commandment demands only that children love and respect their parents, as parents, and not as individuals exercising a role in society. Whatever our father did or did not do in his political functions, in other words, outside of his role as a father to us, not only eludes our understanding but neither engages our responsibility nor asks us to take responsibility. It often happens that children bear the wrongs of their parents, when a wrong has been committed and the children are aware of it. They carry the emotional weight of their pain and shame, but not the responsibility for the wrong. It is often the same for parents, when their children commit a wrong; the parents are not responsible, even if the errors of children can surely be attributed to the parents' education of their children.[14]

The young man struggled to come to terms with his past and his parentage, believing in the impossibility of escaping one's parents "whoever they might be." In 1947, desperate to find some kind of peace, he finally revealed his identity to the village vicar, Father Regens, an erudite, intelligent, and pious man. Martin Adolf had thrown himself into an intensive cate-chism course at the Church of Maria Kirchental, led by Father Regens, who planted the seed of a vocation in him. He helped him through his moral wrestlings and made him a man of God.

Whereas the Nuremberg court had just delivered a death sentence in absentia on his father for war crimes and crimes against humanity, Martin Adolf was finding salvation in God. And whereas Bormann *père* had been a fierce adversary of Christianity, Martin Adolf embraced it wholly, questioning his father's resistance to it. It was Bormann who advocated impos-ing even stricter limits on the Church's authority, in alignment with the views of Hitler who lamented Christianity's weakness: "You see, it's been our misfortune to have the wrong religion. Why didn't we have the religion of the Japanese, who regard sacrifice for the Fatherland as the highest good? The Mohammedan religion too would have been much more compatible to us than Christianity, with its meekness and flabbiness!"[15]

Nevertheless, faced with a hostile population, the Nazis were forced to reign in their attacks on the Church, especially in strongly Catholic regions such as Bavaria; a law passed in 1941, which banned schools from displaying the crucifix on their walls, spurred the population, already exhausted by the war, to resist Nazi policies against the Church.

Martin Adolf found some explanation for his father's devotion to National Socialism when he learned that he ran away from home when he was fifteen to escape his stepfather's bullying and intransigent religiosity. More reasons presented themselves when he examined the ideological conflict between National Socialism and Christianity. His father understood the Church's influence in society as an obvious provocation that had to be suppressed. Since Hitler was the supreme leader of the people, religion contradicted the Führer's superior will. As Hitler's devoted and zealous servant, Bormann took all of Hitler's statements at face value, including this one: "Christianity is an invention of sick brains." The Führer's power was boundless. Bormann certainly had personal reasons as well for his hostility to Christianity, which was an obstacle to his hunger for female conquests.

Martin Adolf believed that no man can ever be forced to renounce his personal convictions to commit a crime, and he was wholly convinced that his father knew of the Nazis' atrocities and that he approved of them.[16] His only explanation for his father's actions was that he was so steeped in the National Socialist ideology that he never questioned it, and that he idolized Hitler as an omnipotent father. Martin Adolf refrained from judging his father, however, believing that to be the prerogative of God, the only fair judge of human behavior. Martin Adolf never discussed his father's actions with him, but he wanted to shoulder responsibility for those crimes nevertheless, even for this man he hardly knew.

Martin Adolf was baptized on May 4, 1947, and received into the Catholic Church of Germany. He enrolled in the secondary school of the Missionaries of the Sacred Heart in Salzburg-Liefering and began theology studies. On October 17, 1947, in a bus to Salzburg for an appointment about his studies, he thought he saw a woman who had been a secretary in the party chancellery in Munich, and that she had recognized him. He was detained the next day and taken before the Counter Intelligence Corps (CIC) of the US Military, then briefly jailed at Zell am See. He learned it was an anonymous tip that had led to his arrest and could not be sure it was the woman in the bus who had denounced him. The archbishop of Salzburg intervened on his behalf and obtained his immediate release. For Christmas that year, Martin Adolf, who was then seventeen, visited his maternal uncle in Ruhpolding, in Bavaria. This uncle, who was living under the name given him by the CIC, "Reinhold Meier," informed him of his mother's death from cancer on March 23, 1946, at the age of thirty-five. On her deathbed, she wished to be reconciled with the Church and receive a Christian burial. She had become close to Theo Schmitz, who was the chaplain at the prison hospital in Merano, who promised to look out for her children.

After the war, Gerda Bormann had been arrested in her house in Gröben, where she had been living with Martin Adolf's nine siblings, who ranged in age from one year to thirteen years. She was taken to Merano by the Allied forces and detained in secret. The children were first baptized as Catholics (even though the oldest had already received the sacrament at birth), then placed with families from a wide swath of society, from aristocrats and doctors to shopkeepers and farmers. Only one of the children, Irmgard, refused to be converted, insisting she wanted to "stay like her father," just like Gudrun Himmler did.

Two of the Bormann children died young. Three-year-old Volker refused to eat and died of malnutrition after several months. One of the older children died as well: Ilse (nicknamed Eicke later), who was taken in by the family of a Merano physician. She was fifteen at the time the Nuremberg court convicted her father, but he remained her hero and she never doubted his innocence. She had both her father's looks and personality; her foster family had its hands full with this adolescent who demanded, ordered, and dominated everyone. At the British school for girls where she was sent, she let her classmates know that they needed to treat her with respect. She was the top student in her class and worked diligently to make her father proud of her. She married an Italian engineer in 1957, and had a daughter but died suddenly at the age of twenty-six.

Different fates awaited the other children. Many of them chose to live in South Tyrol and were rarely in contact with their oldest brother. Martin Adolf entered a Jesuit seminary in Ingolstadt in 1948. In 1951, he earned his secondary school diploma and in July 1958, was ordained a priest. He celebrated his first Mass at the Church of Maria Kirchental.[17] Nevertheless, he lived in constant fear that his father would reappear one day and label him an "enemy," because of his conversion to Catholicism. "I don't hate my father," he has said. "I learned over the course of several years to differentiate between the man who was my father and the man who was a politician and Nazi officer."[18]

There was enormous speculation after the war as to what became of Martin Bormann: the death certificate that was drawn up on May 2, 1945, in the absence of a corpse, was false; he did not commit suicide in the bunker with Hitler but managed to escape. He survived the invasion because he was in reality a KGB agent working for Stalin; the Russian army evacuated him from Berlin, placing a bag over his head to hide his identity. In 1953, there was an alleged sighting of him in Chile. In 1993, the British newspaper the *Independent* published the news that he had been treated for stomach cancer by Josef Mengele, the notorious Auschwitz physician, in Paraguay, before dying on February 15, 1959. Another theory insists that he lived in South America disguised as a priest celebrating marriages, First Communions, and funerals, as well as administering last rites. Martin Adolf lived for years in doubt. Finally, in 1972, excavation work in Berlin uncovered human remains that would be identified as Bormann's thanks to dental records and, in 1988, by DNA testing, although these results have also been contested.

In 1961, Martin Adolf traveled to Africa as a Catholic missionary. He spent years in Congo, which was then in the throes of a civil war, where he was tortured and forced to endure simulated executions. He was not afraid to die, but these traumatizing experiences ruined his health. In late 1965, he returned to Germany for treatment for a contagious disease. At the Institute for Tropical Medicine in Hamburg, he learned from his physician that the son of another Nazi official had recently been treated at the same hospital: Wolf Rüdiger Hess, the son of the party secretary whom his own father replaced at the chancellery in 1941. Both sons had traveled to Africa during the same period but had had radically different experiences there and taken away far different lessons. Martin Adolf returned briefly to Africa in March 1966 but remained for only nine months.

In 1971, he was the victim of a car accident that would open another chapter of his life, and the end of his evangelical mission. Nothing would ever be the same for him again. He attributed his survival to divine intervention, calling it both a "rearranging of the strings of fate" and "a gift of divine providence."[19] When he woke in the hospital, a nurse was at his bedside. She was a nun who had just returned from Ghana where she had been on a mission; it was love at first sight. They were soul mates and became inseparable; nothing would stand in the way of their love. Both renounced their religious vows and were married on November 8, 1971, in Haarlem, in Holland.

In 1973, the same man who had been forbidden from taking catechism class as a boy became a catechism teacher himself. His first application to teach religious education at a school in Mühldorfer was rejected because of his "past history," but he found employment eventually in other institutions.[20]

He taught from 1973 until his retirement in 1992. His wife was an instructor in a religious school in Garmisch-Partenkirchen.

In the 1980s, the Israeli psychologist Dan Bar-On began a study of the children of Nazi criminals to understand how they overcame the wall of silence their parents had built around the past in order to make lives for themselves. He also intended to confront these children with child survivors of the Shoah in the hope that an instructive dialogue could be initiated between them. His reasoning was that Nazi children are also victims, of the guilt they feel because of their fathers' actions. Together these children of both victims and perpetrators of the Holocaust visited Auschwitz and Dachau, as well as the Holocaust museum in Washington, DC, and Yad Vashem in Jerusalem. Martin Adolf was one of the participants. He recognized that he would never have another occasion to discuss the war with his parents, but that the silence he faced was different from the one that torments Holocaust survivors. Theirs is a dark wall behind which lies inexpressible trauma. Parents struggle to find the right words when they want to spare their children the fears and anxiety they suffered, but children can feel both the horror that forces their parents into silence and an obligation to suffer with them.

"I had to keep quiet out of the fear, real or imagined, of being found out and prosecuted as the son of my father, accused of all of the crimes committed by the Nazis, crimes I learned about after the war. I will never have the opportunity to discuss the past with my parents and know what they felt responsible for," Martin Adolf has written.[21]

After he retired, Martin Adolf continued his spiritual journey, undertaking a bible study trip to Israel in 1993, with an ecumenical travel agency for Protestants and Catholics. The theme of the trip was "On the road to *Exodus*." Martin Adolf was fascinated by the country and its people.

He also wrote a document intended for German teachers about how language can be manipulated for the purpose of diffusing propaganda. He based his study on Nazi texts and letters written by his father. For years, he also led workshops with Dan Bar-On in the United States, Germany, and Israel.

His godmother, Ilse Hess, died in 1995. Her son, Wolf

Rüdiger, included this epitaph in her obituary: "The gods flee where destiny begins."[22] He also included a photo of Ilse and Rudolf taken shortly after their marriage; they are seated in a car, with Rudolf at the wheel and Ilse beside him. The look on the groom's face, however, casts an enigmatic pall over the photo. Wolf Rüdiger Hess asked Martin Adolf Bormann to give the eulogy at his mother's funeral; Martin Adolf had visited her twice when she was living in Hidelang. Although they had exchanged letters for years, in which they expressed their disappointment over Rudolf Hess's imprisonment, her funeral was the occasion for the two men to see each other again. This reunion of two children of Nazi criminals brought both of them some happiness.

Martin Adolf Bormann died on March 11, 2013, the same day I began to write his story.

average in all aspects and, as a result, similar to an Eichmann or a Franz Stangl, the executioner at Sobibor and Treblinka. He was the kind of person who could follow the order of a superior officer to kill Jewish men, women, and children, as well as Roma, homosexuals, and "enemies of the state," without the slightest twinge of conscience.

Rudolf Höss was born in 1901 in Baden-Baden, whose natural beauty and thermal baths attracted Germany's high society to the Black Forest. His family was extremely pious, and his father's wish was that his only son become a priest (there were two younger daughters in the family: Maria and Margarete). The Höss family patriarch was a fervent Catholic and an authoritarian father who ruled his children with an iron fist.

He ingrained in Rudolf from a young age the lesson to respect and obey adults, as Rudolf remembered: "Most of all, it was essential to be helpful, and this was my highest duty. It was emphatically pointed out again and again that I carry out the requests and orders of parents, teachers, priests, and all adults, even the servants, and that this principle be respectfully obeyed." He was punished for the slightest mistake. His father's rule of complete obedience to superiors would guide him his entire life. "This type of training is in my flesh and blood," he would write in his journals.[9] He became an adult who would follow orders automatically.

This solitary, withdrawn child was educated to join the priesthood, but his religious convictions were definitively shaken when his confessor reported to his father that Rudolf had been involved in an unremarkable fight at school. For Rudolf, this was nothing less than a monstrous betrayal of his trust; it turned him away from the Church for the rest of his life, and his father's death—in 1914—provided no reason to return. Life as a civilian filled him with anxiety, however, so he chose to become a soldier, like all of the men in his father's family. When World War I broke out, he joined the army. He was fifteen years old.

Germany's defeat left him looking for another military post to satisfy his need for stability. In 1919, he joined the Rossbach Free Corps, operating in East Prussia, as a border guard. This was a nationalist paramilitary group created to fight Communists in the Baltic region, and, with it, Höss would witness for the first time atrocities committed against civilians. He joined the National Socialist party in 1922, as party member 3240. The Rossbach Free Corps was notorious for its brutality, and it would lead Höss to prison. In 1924, he was sentenced to ten years of forced labor in the same murder case involving Martin Bormann, the man who would become Adolf Hitler's personal secretary, and involving the assassination of the Communist Walter Kadow.

Unconditional obedience to the laws of the State was a supreme duty for Höss, as he explained to the Nuremberg psychologist G. M. Gilbert: "[F]rom our entire training the thought of refusing an order just didn't enter into one's head, regardless of what kind of order it was . . ."[10] Would he have killed his own children if he had been ordered to? Höss wished for one thing only: to never have to give an order, only to execute it. This, he believed, exonerated him from any wrongdoing. He was made for prison life with its strict discipline and minutely ordered schedule, and he was a model prisoner, obeying with pleasure.

When he was released four years later from Berlin's Brandenburg Prison, his initial plan was to become a farmer. He contacted the Artamans, a small group of young nationalists promoting a populist ruralism. Höss enjoyed country life, as did Heinrich Himmler, who also joined the group, and it was through the Artamans that Höss met his future wife, Hedwig Hensel, in 1929. They each discovered a soul mate, sharing the same opinions and ideals. Höss had absolute confidence in Hedwig but his innate discipline never allowed him to share his private thoughts with his wife: his problems were his alone to work out.[11] They had five children together: Klaus, who was born three and a half months after their wedding on February 6, 1930; Heidetraut, on April 9, 1932; Inge Brigitt, called Brigitte, on August 18, 1933; Hans-Jürgen in 1937; and Annegret in 1943.

While all around them the German political landscape was changing radically, the family was living quietly on a farm in an isolated region on the Baltic Sea. Rudolf and Hedwig put all their energy into working the land, trying as best they could to meet the needs of their growing family, which counted three children at the time. Despite their idealism, it was a rugged, hard life, and Höss, who had met Himmler in 1929, was eager to accept his invitation to join the SS for active duty. This was in June 1934, when Himmler, as the Reichsführer-SS and in the aftermath of the Night of the Long Knives, had wrested control of the camps from the SS's rival organization, the Nazi Party's Storm Detachment.

In 1934, Höss was assigned to Dachau, the first concentration camp opened by the Nazis, near Munich. The camp's commandant, Thomas Eicke, taught him the first rule of governing the camps: break down the prisoners, mentally and physically. Emblazoned across the top of Eicke's personal stationery was the following phrase: "Only one thing matters: following orders!" His maxim was perfectly in line with Höss's own philosophy. Eicke believed that an SS officer should be prepared to kill his closest family members if they gave cause by refusing the rule of Hitler.[12] Under the direction of Himmler, who thought any emotion was a mark of weakness, the SS became a desensitized, dehumanized security force. Höss had no misgivings about following its lead and falling in step; like a marionette jumping into action on the slightest whim of his superiors, he obeyed orders to the letter. The Nuremberg psychologist Gilbert wrote: "One gets the general impression of a man who is intellectually normal, but with the schizoid apathy, insensitivity and lack of empathy that could hardly be more extreme in a frank psychotic."[13]

The Höss family soon joined him at Dachau; the three children ranged in age from four years to one and a half. The family lived in an officer's house near the camp. In 1937, Hedwig was expecting again, and Hans-Jürgen would become the couple's fourth child and their second son. The Höss children went to the local school in Dachau with the children of other SS officers.

Höss proved what he was capable of at Dachau, which was intended by Himmler to serve as a model for future camps. Höss's formidable efficiency, sense of strategy, and pragmatism moved him up the ranks. Dachau grew to house almost twenty thousand inmates.

Four years later, Höss was transferred to Sachsenhausen, near Berlin, as the camp's second in command. The family moved as well, and their lives were never troubled by the neighboring camp. When war was declared, however, and Poland was invaded on September 1, 1939, prisoners began to stream in.

In the evenings and on weekend afternoons, Höss liked to regale his children with popular German folktales or stories about Max and Moritz, two incorrigible little German pranksters of whom Höss enjoyed in particular. He also played music for them on a gramophone. This good, attentive father was—at the same time—supervising the deliberate deaths of millions of people. For years, he led a double life with ease.

When Himmler decided to open a new camp in Upper Silesia, thirty-seven miles west of Kraków, Höss, who was by this time experienced in the daily functioning of the camps, was part of the delegation sent to inspect the site—a former Polish army barracks on a marshy plain near the Polish town of Oświęcim—in May 1940. Thanks to Höss's efficiency, this new camp, which consisted of twenty-two brick "blocks" arranged in three lines and surrounded by a double perimeter of thirteen-foot-high, barbed-wire enclosures, was ready to receive its first inmates by autumn. The heavy iron gate at the camp's entrance bore the inscription "*Arbeit macht frei*" (Work sets you free).

With the camp up and running, Hedwig and the children joined Rudolf in the house near the camp. As was the case during Höss's earlier postings, the children were sent to the local school. However, Höss's position made it difficult for them to make friends.

The surging numbers of prisoners and Berlin's ever-more insistent demands to build an extension made Höss's life impossible. In the memoirs he wrote while in prison in Poland, he remembered: "Every new problem that appeared lashed me on to even greater intensity."[14] His superiors were unreliable, his subordinates incompetent, and he was frequently faced with logistical difficulties to fulfill his mission, a recurring point of frustration in his memoirs. Höss was the first man to arrive at the camp in the morning and the last to leave in the evening.

Himmler turned a deaf ear to his reports, in which Höss noted a multitude of problems: insufficient supplies, defective machinery, incompetence, and health epidemics among them. Himmler's only concern was to complete the extension of the camp at all costs. After meeting with Himmler at Auschwitz in March 1941, Höss noted: "The following plans for the camp spoke clearly enough: preparation of the camp for 100,000 POWs, the remodeling of the old camp for 30,000 prisoners."[15]

In the autumn of 1941, Höss began work on a second camp, which would become Auschwitz-Birkenau, located about three miles away. This is where the cyanide-based pesticide, Zyklon B, would be tested for use in the gas chambers (it was already in use to decontaminate the barracks) beginning in September 1941. Even a small dose was fatal, and the Nazis had a large stock of it.

Höss recalled that in the summer of 1941[16] Himmler told him: "The Führer has ordered the Endlösung [Final Solution] of the Jewish question—and we have to carry out this task."[17] He explained his reaction to the Nuremberg psychologist, Gilbert: "I had nothing to say; I could only say 'Jawohl!'. . . We could only execute orders without any further consideration. That is the way it was."[18] Auschwitz was chosen for its isolation and its proximity to an existing railway.[19] Höss returned to Auschwitz from that meeting in Berlin with orders to put in place an effective process for large-scale exterminations by gas. It was thought that any other method, especially as used on women and children, would be "a tremendous strain on the SS soldiers who would have to carry out the order."[20] For Höss, "Only gas was suitable since killing by shooting the huge numbers expected would be absolutely impossible."[21] Nevertheless, the extermination kommandos found it increasingly stressful to perform their duties.[22] According to Joachim Fest, it was this mechanization of death that would allow Höss to reject any responsibility or guilt: since he engaged in murder without having the impression he was participating in murder, he was therefore not guilty of murder. What mattered was who gave the order.[23]

Death became Höss's daily companion; his orders were to kill, and he carried them out unfailingly. He was trained to exterminate, then count the dead with a maniacal obsession for numbers and industrial-quality efficiency. In his memoirs, he explains the machinery behind the factory-like extermination of the Jews at Auschwitz, where he was the commandant from 1940 to 1943. It is a dehumanized man who is the author of these pages: he is faithful to his ideals, lays out the obstacles he encountered, and justifies everything he did. In his opinion, pity and compassion were a sign of weakness and had no place in the SS. He recounts his first time observing the use of Zyklon B: "As the gas was thrown in some of them yelled 'Gas!' and a tremendous screaming and shoving started toward both doors, but the doors were able to withstand all the force. It was not until several hours later that the doors were opened and the room aired out. There for the first time I saw gassed bodies in mass. Even though I imagined death by gas to be much worse, I still was overcome by a sick feeling, a horror."[24] He is quick to point out, however, that he never killed a man with his bare hands and never tolerated any abuses by the guards. He also declares himself satisfied that he accomplished the mission given him with tenacious effectiveness.

By 1942, the two camps formed a single, enormous complex, many miles square. Despite his difficulties keeping the guards working efficiently to process inmates through the crematoriums at an ever faster rate, he was proud of his success, for which he was awarded the *Pour le Mérite* cross. Until the end, his only concerns involved the routine problems of the job. Himmler chose Höss over his superiors to create Auschwitz and placed his faith in him, an expression of trust that Höss felt deeply obligated to honor. He wanted to live up to his mission.

The Höss family lived at the camp; a simple wall separated their villa from the gas chambers. The family went about its daily activities, untroubled by what was happening a stone's throw away. Unlike other children of Nazi officials discussed in this book, who were protected from the horrors planned and perpetrated by the Reich—at least until after the war— the Höss children lived next-door to the genocide in progress. Years later, Höss's grandson, Rainer, would call the gate linking the family's yard to the death camp, the "door to Hell."[25]

Höss and his wife were happy together, even if the marriage was passionless. Rudolf's priority was his family's well-being. Although Himmler had forbid him from revealing anything to anyone about the Final Solution, Rudolf broached the matter with Hedwig in late 1942, in the context of his diminished sex drive, which he blamed on the nature of his daily tasks at Auschwitz.[26] Hedwig shared his feelings about the Jewish race and the Polish people, who "only exist to work until they perish."[27]

At home, he continued his efforts to be an exemplary father. Whenever he could, he interrupted his day to play with the children or read them poetry. He was a loving father who deeply regretted not having more time for them.

In addition to two servants who lived in the house, and who were usually Jehovah's Witnesses, the family had a cook, a governess, a painter, a tailor, a seamstress, a barber, and a driver to attend to their daily needs. Hedwig, whose nickname was the "Angel of Auschwitz," insisted a full house staff was necessary to host Reich officials such as Himmler, Adolf Eichmann—who managed the mass deportation of Jews—and Richard Glücks—who was the chief inspector of the camps. The family was especially flattered whenever "Uncle Heini" (Himmler) paid them a visit. Höss photographed the children on these occasions, dressed in their Sunday best and posing on the lap of the Reichsführer.

The family's gardener, Stanislaw Dubiel, was a Polish political prisoner and a privileged observer of the Höss family's private life. In that capacity, the District Commission for Investigation of German Crimes in Poland questioned him on August 7, 1946. He stated that his employers hosted lavish receptions for which he was tasked to appropriate wine, meat, milk, sugar, cocoa, flour, and other foodstuffs, from the camp's warehouse. They lived in a certain opulence for which they paid nothing; Frau Höss was known to be demanding and his job was to satisfy her every whim, taking from the supplies meant for prisoners, if necessary, and all in secret. At the "Canada" shops, which, in camp slang, designated the warehouses where prisoners' personal effects were stored, she took the fine linens and other goods stolen from the women sent to the gas chambers and had them made into clothes for herself by two Jewish seamstresses in her personal service. Dubiel described such a luxuriously appointed and well-equipped house that Frau Höss declared, "I want to live here until I die."[28] After the family fled Auschwitz, four trucks were requisitioned to transport all of the property they had taken for themselves.

Frau Höss's seamstress was thirty-four-year-old Janina

Szczurek, a Pole. In a statement she made on January 13, 1963, she remembered that the lady of the house was always fair with the house staff and the children were no trouble: "They used to run in the garden and watch the prisoners work."[29] Rudolf tucked the children in every night and kissed his wife every morning. He also wrote poetry praising the "beauty of Auschwitz." She recounted one incident that occurred while she worked for the family: "One day they came to me and asked [me] to sew them arm-bands with badges such as the prisoners had. . . . Klaus put on the arm-band of a capo and for the other children I sewed triangles of different colors on their clothes. The children were pleased and as they were running about the garden they met their father who tore off their badges and took them inside. I was not punished but only warned not to do such things."[30]

Rudolf never spoke at home of his work, but to the children he seemed more tired and tense as the years passed. He took it upon himself to oversee the entire extermination process with each new arrival of prisoners, at any hour of the day or night, even watching through a peephole while the prisoners died in the gas chambers.[31] He confided in his memoirs that he was becoming "unapproachable and visibly harder."[32] Yet he tried to keep a calm countenance, knowing that everyone looked to him to set the tone. He wrote that when memories of the horrors he had witnessed at the camp returned to him when he was at home, he could not bear to see the happy scenes of his wife and children together.[33]

His wife attributed his ill humor to occupational stress and told him repeatedly: "Don't always think of your duty, think of your family too."[34] She took him to the theater and to receptions, hoping desperately to brighten his mood, but her efforts were in vain. Rudolf had no appetite for sharing; solitude was his safe haven. He confessed that he never had close family relationships or friendships, even as a boy. He was an island unto himself, and that was enough for him.

The Höss children rarely knew a time when they did not live in proximity to a concentration camp. Brigitte was born on the farm on the Baltic Sea, lived at Dachau for four years beginning at age one, then at Sachsenhausen from age five to seven, and then at Auschwitz from age seven to eleven. The youngest child, Annegret, was born at Auschwitz on September 20, 1943.

Beginning in December 1943, Rudolf Höss was faced with a new challenge. He was appointed head of the Political Department of the Inspectorate of Concentration Camps in the SS Economy and Administration Head Office (SS-WVHA), which oversaw the finances and supply system of the SS as well as the management and inspection of all the concentration camps. He understood his transfer as a consequence of the subdivision of Auschwitz into three separate managing bodies. Others saw it as a move made in the aftermath of an investigation into corruption in the camps or in response to mounting rumors of mass exterminations, which were circulated on British radio. Still others saw an effort to improve productivity in the other camps.[35] Exhausted, Höss requested a six-week leave on grounds of overwork, and he left for the mountains, alone.

Annegret was a little over eight weeks old and she would not see her father again for six months. Hedwig and the children stayed in the villa at Auschwitz. When Rudolf returned in May 1944, he had little time for his family; he had been ordered to exterminate four hundred thousand Hungarian Jews. The crematoriums began working day and night, spreading a dark cloud of ash for miles in all directions.

When Germany fell to the Allies, Höss managed to elude capture for a time. The family—with the exception of Klaus, who stayed with Rudolf—fled north by car, driving at night with the headlights off, following the Himmlers and accompanied by the wife and children of Theodor Eicke. The roads were under constant bombardment by the Allies, forcing them to take shelter in the woods. News of Hitler's death arrived on May 1, 1945.

Like many Nazi Party members and their sympathizers, Höss had planned to commit suicide with his family and had obtained the necessary fatal doses of poison in case of capture by the Russians. He saw no future for them in Germany. He had made his decision clear to Hedwig but they did not carry through because of the children. Later, Höss would regret they turned away from a death that would have spared the family many difficulties and him having to outlive the world he worked so hard to create.[36]

Passing through Berlin, Hedwig and the children stopped in Holstein—in northern Germany—where Rudolf's brother-in-law found them a rudimentary shelter: an old wooden hut with just a stove and a few pieces of furniture. The family slept on the floor with not so much as a blanket. Food was scarce.

Rudolf and Klaus joined Himmler in Flensburg, where the Reich had established a provisional government. Klaus was fifteen: old enough to join the Nazi resistance, at least in the eyes of Rudolf, who was the same age when he enlisted to fight in World War I. They did not expect the news they received from Himmler: "Gentleman, it's over; you know what you have to do." His advice was to hide themselves among the ranks of the Wehrmacht. Höss sent Klaus to his mother, then slipped through British lines and made his way to a German navy outpost on the island of Sylt in northern Germany. After Germany's surrender, he found work on a farm, not far from where Hedwig and the children were hiding. He was able to send letters to them using his brother-in-law as an intermediary, as well as a little money with the help of his former driver at Auschwitz. Nevertheless, the family had only the clothes on their backs and no shoes. They were forced to steal coal to heat the hut and went barefoot in the snow all winter long.

In 1946, Hedwig and the children were living in a small apartment above a sugar factory in the village of St. Michaelisdonn, where, on March 8, she was arrested, leaving the children behind without any supervision. British intelligence officers returned several days later to question the children in the hope of obtaining information that would lead them to their father. According to Brigitte, who was thirteen, they screamed at the children, "Where is your father? Where is your father?" The children claimed to know nothing, so the officers imprisoned Klaus along with his mother.

Hedwig was threatened with deportation to Siberia if she did not cooperate with the investigation into Rudolf's whereabouts. After at first insisting that he was dead, she finally cracked and gave them his assumed name, "Franz Lang," and told them where to find him.

Shortly thereafter, on March 11, 1946, Rudolf Höss was captured on a farm near Flensburg. His cyanide vial had broken several days earlier, leaving him no choice but to give himself up. He would testify at Nuremberg as a defense witness for Ernst

Kaltenbrunner, chief of Reich Security, whose lawyer hoped to prove that Kaltenbrunner had never visited Auschwitz nor signed any execution orders. However, Höss's testimony was immensely damning, and Höss himself said later that he never understood why he had been called as a witness. The Nuremberg psychologist G. M. Gilbert asked him if he felt the Jews had deserved to die. Höss answered: "We SS men were not supposed to think about these things, it never occurred to us. And besides, it was something already taken for granted that the Jews were to blame for everything."[37]

As a prisoner of the British army, Höss was transferred to the Polish authorities and tried by Poland's Supreme National Tribunal beginning in March 1947. He was a model prisoner as well as a model defendant: he answered questions with extreme precision and never made any attempt to whitewash his answers, probably because he did not appreciate the enormity of his actions. He testified he had long ago stopped feeling any emotion. In the eyes of this ardent National Socialist, Auschwitz was no different than the bombing of German cities. Höss was in complete agreement with the Weltanschauung of National Socialism, a philosophy "uniquely linked to the character of the German people" and "able to lead them gradually back to a lifestyle in harmony with nature."[38] His memoirs close on these dumbfounding words: "May the general public simply go on seeing me as the bloodthirsty beast, the cruel sadist, the murderer of millions, because the broad masses cannot conceive the Kommandant of Auschwitz in any other way. They would never be able to understand that he also had a heart . . ."[39]

On the eve of his death, he confided that his family was as dear to him as National Socialism: "Worrying about their future is always uppermost in my mind. The farm was supposed to be

GUDRUN HIMMLER
Nazism's "Poppet"

Heinrich Himmler, his daughter
Gudrun (*front, middle*), his
adopted son, and a friend, 1935

Gudrun and Margaret Himmler,
daughter and wife of the SS chief,
Heinrich Himmler

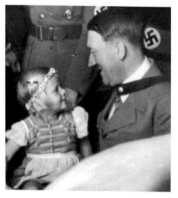

Gudrun Himmler and
Adolf Hitler

Gudrun and her father, Heinrich
Himmler, at Dachau concentration
camp, 1941

EDDA GÖRING
The Little Princess of "The Nero of Nazi Germany"

Edda and Hermann Göring, 1940

Baptism of Edda Göring. The wife of
Hermann Göring with Adolf Hitler,
the child's godfather

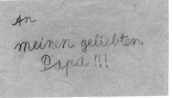

A letter written by Edda
Göring to her father in
Nuremburg

A page from Hermann Göring's
personal photo album

Edda and her mother
arriving at Nuremberg to
visit Hermann Göring,
September 1946

WOLF R. HESS
A Life in the Shadow of the Last of the War Criminals

Rudolf Hess and Wolf Rüdiger Hess

NIKLAS FRANK
A Hunger for Truth

Family photos

Niklas, his mother, and his sister arriving at Nuremberg to visit Hans Frank, September 1946

Martin Adolf Bormann Jr.
"The Crown Prince"

Martin Adolf Bormann Jr. in his school uniform at Feldafing, 1943

Martin Adolf Bormann Jr. in his cassock after becoming a Catholic priest, 1958

The Bormann children

The Höss Children
The Family of the Kommandant of Auschwitz

The Höss family

The Höss children playing in their garden
at Auschwitz

The Speer Children
The Offspring of "The Devil's Architect"

Albert Speer with his five children

Adolf Hitler with three of
the Speer children at the
Berghof

ROLF MENGELE
The Son of "The Angel of Death"

Josef Mengele and
his son Rolf in the
mountains, 1956

Josef Mengele, hiding from the
Allies in southern Germany,
with his son Rolf, 1947

our homestead. My wife and I saw in the children our purpose in life. It was to be our life's task to enable them to get a good education and create a stable home life for them. . . . As far as I am concerned, I have written myself off right from the beginning. I do not worry about this anymore. I am finished with it. But my wife, my children?"[40] He was executed by hanging on April 16, 1947, at Auschwitz, about 150 feet from the family's former home.

Höss wrote a final letter to his wife and children dated April 11, 1947. In it, he urges Hedwig to move as far away as possible and to use her maiden name because "it's better that my name dies with me." To the children, he wrote, "Your daddy has to leave you now." For his eldest son, Klaus, he had these words: "Klaus, my dear boy! You are the oldest. You are now going out into the world. You have to now make your own way through life. You have good aptitudes. Use them! Keep your good heart. Become a person who lets himself be guided primarily by warmth and humanity. Learn to think and to judge for yourself, responsibly. Don't accept everything without criticism and as absolutely true."[41]

Impoverished, the family kept a low profile and tried to make a clean slate of life.[42] Hedwig and the children lived for ten years in St. Michaelisdonn where they were eventually accepted into the community, although not by everyone. As the widow of a war criminal, she was not eligible for a pension or any government support. The children moved away as adults: Klaus to Australia, others to the Baltic countries, Brigitte to the United States.

In 1950, Brigitte, the third of the five children, left Germany for Spain. She was a beautiful blonde and found work as a fashion model for Balenciaga. She also met her future husband, an Irish American working in Washington, DC. It was at this same time that her father's memoirs were published, a confession that will go down in the annals of history. She lived successively in Liberia, Greece, Iran, and Vietnam, following the career of her husband (the couple married in 1961) with whom she had a son and a daughter. Brigitte shared her family history with her future husband shortly after they met; he expressed some shock but came to the conclusion from their talks that she was a victim, a child at the time of the events whose life shifted from privilege to poverty from one day to the next.

In 1972, the couple moved to northern Virginia but Brigitte was uncomfortable in these new surroundings, without friends, any marketable skills—she admitted she was incapable of writing a check—or fluency in English. She found work as a part-time salesclerk, where her sense of fashion prompted a Jewish client to suggest she go to work at Saks Jandel, a designer clothing store catering to the Washington elite. Not long after starting in this new job, she got drunk with the store's manager and told him that her father was none other than Rudolf Höss, the Kommandant of Auschwitz. The manager relayed the information to the store's owners, who were German Jews who had emigrated to the United States after Kristallnacht in 1938. They chose not to fire Brigitte who, in their estimation, had committed no crime herself.

Brigitte would learn of their discretion many years later; she continued to work at Saks Jandel for thirty-five years, where the owners treated her as an individual in her own right, not as "the daughter of . . ." They never revealed her secret to anyone. Brigitte hid her identity from friends and acquaintances, saying only that her father died during the war. She struggled with the question of revealing her father's identity to her grandchildren. When her mother died in 1989, she had her buried under an assumed name.

After Brigitte and her husband divorced, she moved closer to Washington, DC, to live with her son, a jazz pianist. Her daughter had died of cancer, and Brigitte was similarly diagnosed. In 2013, she granted an interview[43] to Thomas Harding for his book, *Hanns and Rudolf*, about Höss's capture after the war by Harding's great-uncle, Hanns Alexander, a German Jew. She requested that neither her married name nor her maiden name be used, or any other personal information that could lead to her identification, fearing possible retaliatory measures against her or her family.

She agreed to the interview because of her advanced age. Although she had always kept her secret to herself, it no longer seemed impossible to her that one of her descendants could do something horrible. After the war, she at first denied her father's involvement, then minimized his role, stressing that Auschwitz was not her father's idea and that he acted under orders of Himmler and Hitler. Moreover, he was an exemplary father and "the nicest man in the world." Harding asked her how that could be when he was responsible for millions of deaths at Auschwitz. She claimed not to know, but, she also argued, "There must have been two sides to him. The one that I knew and then another. . . ." She also questioned the official number of Jews sent to their deaths: "How can there be so many survivors if so many had been killed?" She explained her father's confession as a statement made under torture and showed the journalist her parents' wedding photo, which she kept over her bed. As for her nephew, Rainer Höss, she has called him "an unbelievable liar."[44]

Rainer Höss is the son of Hans-Jürgen, the second son of Rudolf Höss. When Rainer was twelve, he learned that his grandfather was one of the "worst mass murderers in history," and it changed him forever.

Rainer's father shared the ideas of his own father. Rainer remembers Hans-Jürgen as a violent, anti-Semitic dictator at home. Like his sister Brigitte, Hans-Jürgen resisted sharing his secret with his son. Every attempt Rainer made to question him was met with silence, and he would only learn of his family history after a gardener at the boarding school he attended— an Auschwitz survivor—regularly mistreated him on the basis of his family name. "He beat me because he projected onto me all of the suffering he endured," Rainer explained. "A Höss is always a Höss, whether you are the grandfather or the grandson: guilty."[45]

This heavy silence draped itself over many families. Rainer Höss decided to uncover the secrets on his own, searching in archives and on the Internet for any information he could find about his grandfather. He gathered photos of a smiling, happy family on the grounds of the villa at Auschwitz. His mother, Irene, divorced his father after twenty-seven years of marriage. Hans-Jürgen had never told her that he was the son of Rudolf Höss; she read about it in the newspaper. She said he never talked about Auschwitz except when he was feeling melancholic.

Rainer Höss has struggled to live with his family history. He twice attempted suicide as a teenager. He has had three heart attacks and suffers from asthma, which has worsened over time as he has dedicated himself to researching his past. Unlike the other members of his family, however, he has not turned a blind eye to his family's history and considers that if his grandfather was a mass murderer, then shame and sadness are just his lot in life.

The rest of the Höss family has declared him a traitor and refuses to have any contact with him. For his part, he severed all ties in 1985.[46] His goal in pursuing his research is to prevent this buried past from coming back to haunt his children. Over the years, he has ceased to feel personally responsible but still feels burdened by the past.

Nevertheless, to understand Rainer Höss is to know he is a controversial figure. He attempted to sell some of his grandfather's personal effects to the Yad Vashem Holocaust Museum, an act that earned him opprobrium as a macabre mercantilist. He addressed a brief letter to the museum authorities: "Rare objects, Auschwitz Kommandant Höss. Certain personal effects of Rudolf Höss, the Kommandant of Auschwitz: a large fire-resistant chest bearing official insignia—a gift from Heinrich Himmler, SS Chief—weighing 50 kg, a paper-cutter, never-before seen files and photos of Auschwitz, letters dating from his detention in Kraków. Request the pleasure of a response. Cordially, Rainer Höss."[47] He has denied the affair, using two different defenses: first, that the letter was written by the son of another Nazi official, and, later, that it was Yad Vashem that contacted him, and not vice versa.

When he introduces himself, he has said, he can see people's distrust in their eyes, as if he had the same diabolical nature as his grandfather. He never sought to change his name, however, feeling it would have no effect. He arranged to meet Jozef Paczynski, a concentration camp survivor who was his grandfather's barber, hoping to have a constructive, well-intentioned conversation with him. Paczynski asked him to stand up so he could get a good look at him, then declared him the spitting image of his grandfather. When people ask him about his grandfather, Rainer likes to repeat what he said during a visit to Auschwitz: "If I knew where my grandfather was buried, I would piss on his grave."[48]

In 2014, Rainer Höss appeared in a video for the European Parliament campaign of the Swedish Social Democratic Party, which was fighting the rise of extremism in Europe with the slogan: "Never forget to vote." By Rainer's analysis, the far-right parties are better organized today than they were in Nazi Germany, and he fears that Europe has not learned its lesson.

THE SPEER CHILDREN

The Offspring of "The Devil's Architect"

It is an August evening in Frankfurt in 2013. Albert is studying a model built to his specifications for EXPO 2000 in Hanover. Measuring five feet by five feet, the model is a clue to the sheer size of the project. Albert likes to describe it in every last detail, in all of its elegance. He would say, however, that he doesn't have a style, as if he didn't have any influences. He has been designing buildings since 1964, when he won his first architecture prize for his proposal for a new train station in Ludwigshafen, Germany. He was thirty when he entered that anonymous competition. He carries his father's first and last names—Albert Speer—and he believes that if the jury had known who he was, things might have turned out differently, but he tries not to think about it. He does know, however, that his father would have been proud of him that day.

The dying sunset is reflected on the glass skyscraper where he has his office. His father always worked in stone; Albert prefers materials such as glass that give an impression of weightlessness. He and his team are always searching for creative solutions; creativity is not only their motto but his driving motivation. When his colleagues question the size of the buildings he wants to design, he always answers that they should never be afraid to dream big. Size alone is not synonymous with greatness.

On the threshold of his eighties, he can look back on his life and see that he was always a dreamer; he would choose the unpredictable over the ordinary any day. His ambitions have taken him all over the world: his architecture firm, AS&P, has had offices in Asia for many years with countless operations.

Today, he is dreaming about the desert and remembering the presentation he made in Doha, Qatar. Standing before a huge multimedia screen, he made buildings appear and disappear as he presented his proposal for Qatar's bid to host the FIFA World Cup in 2022. People said his project was crazy; it would be the most freakish construction in the history of architecture. His answer: "Major events like the Olympics or the World Cup make the unthinkable thinkable."[1] In the book he published in 1992, *Die intelligente Stadt* (*The Intelligent City*),[2] he outlined his vision for a forward-thinking, people-centered metropolis whose sole function is to make its inhabitants happy. For Speer, a city should feel natural and spontaneous: its human dimension should never be underestimated. The hallmarks of its creator should also be invisible; his plans are only a framework for others to work from: their realization is up to the architects, the designers, and the builders.[3] He is more interested in cities and their complexities than by the aesthetics of individual buildings. He thinks of himself above all as a designer of urban spaces.

His wife enters, and Albert Speer Jr. gets up from his desk, turns off his desk lamp, then takes a look to see that all the lights are off in the office. It is a natural gesture for this man credited with pioneering the concept of "sustainability" in urban planning. He has even been called "the green conscience of the industry."[4]

With Ingmar Zeisberg, his wife since 1972, he leaves the building. Ingmar is an actress and Albert's only love for over forty years. As the couple walks through Frankfurt's streets at night, he reflects on the role he has played in the city's development. For Speer, no other German city rivals Frankfurt for internationalism: a global model. Here, too, he is better known as an architect than as the son of his father, another famous architect in Germany. Whereas his father left his mark on Berlin, Albert feels most at home in Frankfurt, the "Jewish city" that Hitler despised. In Frankfurt, he is the star architect, not his father. Working in separate cities also helps Albert avoid drawing comparisons between their respective accomplishments. In any case, Berliners don't seem ready to have another Speer designing the city's architecture: his proposals have always been refused on the same grounds: "Speer in Berlin? We've tried that already."[5]

In preparation for the Olympic Games in Beijing in 2008, China wanted to show off on a grand scale. In 2002, the city solicited architectural firms, including AS&P, for designs for a project linking the Forbidden City to the new stadium. The grandiose project submitted by Speer's firm was not without similarities to his father's design for the Berlin Olympic stadium in 1936, or "Germania," the capital of Nazi Germany imagined by Hitler and designed by Albert Speer Sr.

That project proposed a North-South / East-West layout

and a major reorganization of the city's railway. There was to be a wide central axis known as the Avenue of Splendors that would lead north to the Volkshalle, a huge, domed monument inspired by the Roman Pantheon; to the south would lie the headquarters of the Wehrmacht. The east and west axes were to terminate, respectively, in the German Parliament, known as the Reichstag, and a new chancellery and palace for the Führer.

A British newspaper wrote that AS&P's project was inspired by Germania,[6] an allegation that still troubles Albert Speer Jr. as he walks the streets of Frankfurt. Others think he is driven by an unconscious desire to distance himself from his father. Comparisons are inevitable when father and son practice the same profession. At his age, however, he is tired of being "the son of . . . ." Nevertheless, and despite being named after his father, he never thought to take an alias. What matters to him is that people consider him an architect in his own right, and his creations in the same way. As far as he is concerned, he is a self-made man.[7]

On his personal web page, www.albertspeer.de, Speer outlines three generations of architects going back to his grandfather, Albert Freidrich. He describes his father, Albert, as an "architect/politician" and himself, Professor Albert Speer, as an "architect/urban planner." His research for the site led him to search through boxes of old photos in the family home in the Allgäu that his father loved so much. In an early version of the site, he imagined what each Speer's favorite project would have been. For his grandfather, he chose a renovated building in the historic quarter of Mannheim. For his father, it was the Reich Chancellery, which was the Führer's official residence in central Berlin from 1938 to 1945. As for his own best work, he chose his design for Europaviertel, a district in Frankfurt. He began the project in 2005 and considers it the crowning glory of his illustrious career. The website included a personal and professional timeline entitled "La Dolce Vita," with a photo of his father, Hitler's architect, surrounded by his children. The photo was taken at Obersalzberg on the magnificent slopes of the Bavarian Alps. During a subsequent update of the site, all images of his father were removed.

The photo was a memory of his happy childhood in the mountains, surrounded by forests and wildlife. That was before the truth caught up with his family and he became the son of "the Devil's architect," before his father was jailed at Spandau Prison in Berlin, and after he was found guilty of war crimes and crimes against humanity. He remembers that he was twelve at the time and that he suffered from a stuttering problem, which poisoned his adolescence and troubles him still today. He cannot remember when it began exactly but he admits his condition is probably "linked to all that."[8] To overcome his handicap, the best medicine was to do what he hated most: talk and talk and talk.[9]

The Speer family moved onto Hitler's mountain in 1938, where the close relationship between Hitler and his architect was reinforced by their physical proximity. Albert Speer joined the ranks of Nazi officials like Göring, the Reichsmarschall, and Bormann, Hitler's personal secretary who lived comfortably on large properties near the Führer's Berghof. Hitler had a spacious architecture studio built for Speer so he could work whenever he wanted. The family took over a house that had belonged previously to a painter, Bormann having evicted the local population to make room for Hitler's inner circle.

Albert Jr. was born in Berlin in 1934. Five children followed: Hilde (1936), Fritz (1937), Margret (1938), Arnold (1940), and Ernst (1942). As their father rose rapidly to prominence, his absences from home increased. Hitler had a passionate interest in architecture, and the two men were destined to meet. For Speer, architecture opened the door to the center of the Third Reich's power structure, a fact he would nevertheless attempt to nuance later: "I felt myself to be Hitler's architect. Political events did not concern me. My job was simply to provide impressive backdrops."[10] He also showed little consideration for the millions of forced laborers he sent to work on his monumental projects.

Speer distinguished himself among the rest of the minds behind the Nazi machine in that he was one of the few, if not the only, Nazi official with a brilliant intellect. How could such an individual support the Nazi agenda and its murderous persecution of the Jews? Why did he serve the regime to the last? Without Speer, Germany likely would have lost the war earlier. At least, that is the conclusion of historians like Hugh Trevor-Roper, who have called Speer "the real criminal of Nazi Germany."[11]

Albert Speer Sr. was a child of the Black Forest. He was born in 1905 in Mannheim into an architect's family, whose comfortable existence protected him from the changes sweeping the world. He was a small, scrawny child, with little tolerance for physical exertion, due to a nervous system disorder that was diagnosed when he was very young. He compensated for his physical weakness by developing his mental agility, and at the age of twelve he drew his first artwork with India ink.

At the age of seventeen, he fell in love with Margarete

Weber, a girl he met on his way to school one day. She was the daughter of a cabinetmaker, and Albert's parents judged her an insufficient match for their son. Albert payed no attention and married her six years later; his parents were not invited to the wedding. Much to his father's pleasure, however, Albert gave up his earlier plan to study mathematics and took up architecture studies instead, first in Munich and then at the Technical University of Berlin-Charlottenburg, where—in 1927—he became the assistant to Heinrich Tessenow. This architect and urban planner was one of the most active architects during the Weimar Republic and a prominent member of the German Arts and Crafts movement. Speer followed in his father's footsteps, as his son would follow in his.

The Speers were a liberal family with little interest in politics. Albert discovered National Socialism by way of an analogy drawn between the party's ideology and the theories of his mentor, Tessenow, who believed that "style emanates from the people."[12] Speer wrote later that Tessenow, who rejected Nazism, would have been horrified by this comparison.[13] Hitler was gaining a following among students, and it was at a speech he delivered at the Technical University that Speer fell under the "almost hypnotic impression" Hitler left on him, writing later: "His persuasiveness, the peculiar magic of his by no means pleasant voice, the oddity of his rather banal manner, the seductive simplicity with which he attacked the complexity of our problems—all that bewildered and fascinated me. I knew virtually nothing about his program. He had taken hold of me before I had grasped what was happening."[14]

Albert was not the only member of his family who rallied to National Socialism early on; his mother was favorably impressed by the party's promise of "discipline in a time of chaos."[15] She joined the party but never told her husband, whose aversion to politics she knew well, but she would share her secret years later with her son.

After several years as Tessenow's assistant, during which his salary was cut due to the economic crisis in Germany, Speer began to look around for an opportunity to open his own architecture office in his hometown of Mannheim. This was in 1931, and Speer was twenty-six. The economic situation convinced him to bide his time: the chances of a young, inexperienced architect finding work would be extremely slim, at a time when the country was experiencing unprecedented hyperinflation and construction was at a standstill.

Since he owned an automobile, he proposed his services to the National Socialist Motor Corp, the NSKK, and was named president of the organization's office in Wannsee, the Berlin suburb where he lived. Karl Hanke, who was then a regional party official, hired Speer to renovate the regional party offices in Berlin, which were subsequently named after Adolf Hitler. Hanke was sufficiently satisfied with the result to recommend Speer to his superiors.

After Hitler was named Reich Chancellor, Joseph Goebbels, the Reich Minister of Propaganda, turned to Speer to work on the party's headquarters in Berlin. However, it was his set design for the Nazi rally on May 1, 1933, on the Tempelhof esplanade that made a lasting impression on the party's high command. Speer proposed an enormous platform to be erected in front of three flags, each the height of a six-story building, with the middle flag flying the Nazi swastika. The entire scene would be illuminated by one hundred and thirty powerful military searchlights to create an "ice cathedral."[16] The success of his vision for that event led him to design the set for the

Nuremberg Rally that same year. In Speer, the party found the man who could translate the future power of the new Germany under Hitler into visible form. Hitler was sold. Speer learned at their first meeting that the word "architecture" held an almost magical power over the Führer.

During the renovation of the chancellery, Speer was named assistant to Paul Ludwig Troost, who was Hitler's chief architect at the time. In his new position, he was responsible for providing regular updates on the work's progress to the Führer. One day, Hitler invited him to lunch and explained that he was looking for a young architect who could realize the architectural vision of the new Germany. Albert Speer was his man. Troost's death in 1934 accelerated Speer's rendezvous with destiny; he was subsequently named head of the Chief Office for Construction: effectively the chief architect of the Reich.

At Obersalzberg, near the Austrian border, life followed its course. Every year for Hitler's birthday, the children put on their Sunday best, and everyone helped the Führer blow out the candles on his chocolate birthday cake at his mountain chalet, the Berghof. Each child presented him with a bouquet of flowers, then a photo was taken of Hitler surrounded by his little admirers. Eva Braun, Hitler's mistress, made a number of short films where a smiling Hitler can be seen playing with the children. The Speer children appear in these films, playing with Martin Bormann's children and Göring's daughter. When Albert Jr. watched one such film showing him and his sister with the Führer, he recalled a particularly pleasant man who was like a gentle uncle with the children. His own father remembered, however, that children did not usually gravitate toward Hitler who "never found the proper easy manner of treating them; after a few benign words he would soon turn to others."[17]

Such was the life of the Speer children during the war; a tranquil existence in a magnificent alpine setting, far removed from the war's privations and protected from strangers and intruders. Until April 25, 1945, not a single bomb fell there. From their villa, they had a panoramic view of the Watzmann mountain, one of the highest peaks in Germany, which towers over Obersalzberg. The Speer children who were old enough attended the local school in Berchtesgaden with the other children living on the vast private estate reserved for Nazi officials. Every morning, they walked the almost four miles to the village, about an hour's walk, and returned the same way. Albert Jr. remembered that he hated school because he was always told what to do.[18] There was no evidence of National Socialism in the Speer home, not a single uniform, symbol, or ritual. His sister Margret would recall a childhood completely different from what the Bormann children knew, who were raised by fanatical parents according to the tenants of the party's ideology.

Speer was a man who had everything, including a happy family life. He was an elegant man who abhorred the coarseness and boorishness of someone like Martin Bormann, who brought his mistress to live with his wife and children. Margret remembers a happy childhood; her father had a certain sense of humor and was not particularly authoritarian. On that last point, however, Albert Jr. does not entirely agree with her.

Living at Obersalzberg had its inconveniences. Hitler entertained incessantly, and Speer was obligated to attend these dull evenings on a regular basis when he might have been making progress on his designs. Speer was a workhorse, and nothing made him happier than to spend day and night on his plans.

Hitler expected to see him at every event, however, and Speer admitted that if Hitler had had any close friends, he would have been counted among them.[19] Aware of the rivalries and conflicts that absorbed his subordinates, Hitler appreciated Speer as someone who knew how to steer clear of these plots and stay focused on his work. After he was named Minister of Armaments in 1942, Speer decided to skip the Christmas holidays with his family, preferring to spend them alone in Lapland. His wife had to make do in his absence.

In April 1945, Speer could feel the tide turning and knew that this idyllic chapter of their life was coming to a close. The children were heartbroken to leave Berchtesgaden and sensed that something was afoot, without knowing what or how big. Speer knew he was risking Hitler's ire by leaving: anyone who abandoned the Führer was a traitor in his eyes. Speer saw no other solution, however, and the family headed north to flee the advance of the Allies and to join the Reich's provisional government, which would be led after Hitler's death by Karl Dönitz. Speer made it that far, but was arrested with the other members of the Flensburg government on May 23, 1945.

After their comfortable mountain villa, the family of seven was forced into a cramped, two-room apartment. The children had been baptized, like those of many other party leaders. Their job at present was to blend in despite their father's absence and status as a war criminal,[20] which had consequences for all of them. So began a long journey for the Speer children, one that would radically change their relationships with their father and make communication with him difficult. It was no different for Albert Jr. even though he had an obvious subject in common with his father. He may have considered that—as an architect—he was following in his grandfather's footsteps as much as his father's.

Speer was transferred from the prison at Mondorf-les-Bains to Luxembourg, and from there to Versailles, and finally to Nuremberg to await his trial in late 1945. The family went to live in the house of Speer's parents in Heidelberg in the Black Forest, which provided them a comfortable home. The children had had to interrupt their schooling for a year but were able to enroll in the Heidelberg public schools, after initial resistance due to their parentage. Margarete and Albert were both Heidelberg natives, a fact that eased the family's transition into life in this small town.

Some of the children's teachers also chose to look the other way. One of Albert's instructors lectured the class: "You all know what has become of the father of one of your classmates. This is precisely why I would like you to behave yourselves correctly with him."[21] Nevertheless, he struggled in school and, when he was fifteen, was offered a carpenter's apprenticeship. His road to becoming an architect would be hard, but there would be many successes. After three years of study and night classes, he eventually earned his secondary school diploma and enrolled at the Technical University of Munich to begin architecture studies under Hans Döllgast, a major postwar architect who had received the Heinrich Tessenow Gold Medal in 1972, named, of course, for Albert's father's mentor.

Albert's two sisters, Hilde and Margret, attended a Protestant boarding school for girls near Heidelberg, named after the wartime resistance fighter, Elisabeth von Thadden. The girls' identity was not a secret to their classmates or their teachers, yet the sisters integrated easily and would be forever grateful for the generosity of spirit they were shown there. Hilde would later pay homage to her history teacher, Dora Lux, a survivor of a Jewish family living in Berlin during the war, for her intellectual guidance.[22] Margret became friendly with a certain Adda, the daughter of Hans Bernd von Haeften, who was a member of the German resistance involved with the July 20, 1944, assassination plot against Hitler. Adda's father was hanged as a traitor by the Nazis; Margret's father was a war criminal and still alive. For the first time, she felt guilty as the "bad" child of a Nazi criminal, compared to her friend, the "good" daughter of a hero of the resistance. As for Arnold, the fifth of the six Speer children, his relationship with his father would never be the same: "Until 1945, he was my father and I could look him in the eye; after 1945, he was a war criminal."[23]

At Nuremberg, Albert Speer created an elaborate defense that rested on his condemnation of the ideology of the Nazis and their Führer, but also, as pertaining to his functions as an influential figure within the regime, on the notion of "collective responsibility for all the measures of Hitler."[24]

He was indicted on four counts and acquitted on two: conspiracy and crimes against peace. On October 1, 1946, he was sentenced to twenty years in prison for war crimes and crimes against humanity. During the trial, Speer's attitude and his recognition of both guilt and collaboration, by which he tried to distance himself from his codefendants, worked in his favor. In a further effort to argue for a lenient sentence, he also testified that he had hatched a plot to kill Hitler and that he was one of the few members of Hitler's inner circle who voiced opposition to his scorched earth policy. According to his biographer Gitta Sereny,[25] Speer would not have helped his case by expressing any doubt about the regime's treatment of the Jews, as doing so would have implied knowledge of the persecution and geno-cide, which would have made him a de facto cog in the death machine. Speer stuck therefore to a clever line of defense, helped by the fact that certain writings of his that would have been damning had not yet come to light.

Speer was forty-one at the time of his sentence. He did the math in his prison diary: "I'll be sixty-one when I am released. . . . It is as if I am entering an immeasurably long tunnel."[26] Speer need not have feared the boredom of incar-ceration: this cold, unfeeling man proved adept at suppressing inconvenient memories and emotions, a technique that would prove useful during the long years of his sentence. He immedi-ately created a charity fund to support his family—with the help of his trusted childhood friend, Rudolf Wolters, and former contacts of Speer's—to which donations were made with the promise of return favors. Through the fund, the family received a monthly stipend of two hundred deutschmarks.[27] All told, Speer was able to raise over five hundred thousand deutsch-marks between 1948 and 1966 when he was released. At the time he began his sentence, his children ranged in age from one and a half to eleven and a half years. Speer also put into place a system of financial incentives to encourage his children to earn high marks in school, another way Speer continued to rule over his family, even from his prison cell. Margarete, with six children to raise by herself, did not hesitate to call upon Wolters as needed. Wolters also created a communication sys-tem, a sort of secret line, by which Speer could communicate freely with the outside world, sharing the abundant notes he took on his activities and thoughts.

In fact, writing quickly became the principal activity of pris-oner "Five," as he was known within Spandau; he wanted to "tell all," whether about himself or about Hitler. However, he quickly abandoned the biography of Hitler he had begun in order to concentrate his efforts on himself. As Rudolf Hess did with his family, Speer also refused visits from his wife and children in prison, for eight years. Was it, as he wrote in his prison journals, to avoid seeing his children cry at the end of each visit?[28] The oldest were adolescents when they were first allowed at Spandau, in 1953.

These half-hour, monthly visits were tiresome and rote. Speer had little to say to the children as he stood stiffly before them, a smile screwed to his face. He found impersonal questions to ask them to fill the lulls in the conversation, and they answered politely. He felt as though they "exchanged monologues" and he wondered if he had "lost them not just for the duration of [his] detention, but forever."[29] He felt as if he did not even know who they were. Before his capture, his relentless schedule kept him away from home. "He very rarely saw his family," Margarete remembered.[30]

With time on his hands at Spandau, however, he did think about the children, and shared his thoughts in his letters. For his children, these opened the door to some understanding of their father, although for some of them he would remain a perfect stranger. Their relations were formal; they exchanged no physical gestures nor displays of warmth, only the usual courtesies. The children even refrained from calling him "father." Speer wondered at times if "it might be better if I never came home again."[31] Margret would remember that when it was time to write to him, the whole family would gather to scrupulously choose every word.[32] They sent photographs with every letter so he could see how much they had grown, but he could barely tell them apart.[33] He put great effort into maintaining a semblance of a relationship with them, composing gay, comical stories about his childhood and about life in prison. Hilde, who was the second child in the family and the eldest daughter, remembers these letters often made her laugh heartily.

Hilde was Speer's biggest and best ally. Ever loyal to him, she took it upon herself to act as a liaison between her father and his circle of supporters, and every year she wrote to the office of the German president requesting, in the name of her entire family, that her father be released. Her letters were well received, and Charles de Gaulle and Willy Brandt counted themselves among her father's supporters.[34] Nevertheless, Speer's sentence was never commuted. Brandt was the mayor of Berlin when Speer was finally released and he sent Hilde a bouquet of red roses to congratulate her. Speer was also spared a denazification trial—during which his property would have been confiscated—for which he had Brandt to thank.

Hilde was probably Speer's favorite child, the one who made him the happiest, but as a female, she could never be his confidante; for Speer, that role could only be held by a son, a man like himself. He began an intimate correspondence with Ulf Schramm, Hilde's husband, because he felt it stimulated him intellectually to do so, but it eventually overshadowed his need to communicate with the rest of his family, so that he only shared practical news with them.[35]

When she was sixteen, Hilde was refused a visa to study in the United States under a student grant program. Her case was the object of sufficient publicity—including from an Israeli family who hoped to host her—for the American government to reverse its decision. Speer was never reassured however by the idea of his daughter studying in America, fearing she would be treated badly as the daughter of a German war criminal.

Hilde wrote her father a letter, dated May 13, 1953, in which, for the first time, she asked him about his participation in Nazi atrocities. He responded with a long letter in which he told her: "And just to calm you, of the dreadful things, I knew nothing."[36] He suggested that she might understand better if she read G. M. Gilbert's *Nuremberg Diary* in which the psychologist recorded Speer's interpretation of events: "He knew no more about concentration camps than any other minister knew about V-2."[37]

Speer's relations with the youngest of his children, Ernst, were the most difficult. Ernst was not yet two when Speer was imprisoned, and the little boy never said a word during his visits to Spandau. Withdrawn and taciturn, he refused to speak of his father for the rest of his life, saying only, "I had nothing to say to him. It's sad, but that was always the case."[38] However, in 1968, Ernst, his wife, and their two children moved into a garage adjacent to the Speer property in Heidelberg. "I knew my father only as a stranger," he admitted, and summarized his relationship as having a father and not having one at the same time.[39] Things were no easier between Speer and his third child, Fritz, even though Speer found Fritz to be very intelligent and the one who resembled him the most. In his prison journal, he confided his irritation at his son's seriousness and embarrassment, which rendered the boy speechless and unable to answer his father's questions. As for Arnold, his third son, he found nothing more interesting to discuss than the furnishings in the visiting room: there was no emotional contact between them.[40]

Speer spent his prison sentence usefully, defending his reputation, writing his life story, and explaining Hitler's influence on him. His antidote to depression was writing, a process he thought of as "liberation by writing things down."[41] He tried his hand at gardening and walked in the prison yard. He developed a method for distracting himself by imagining walking around the entire world; between 1953 and 1966, he walked between 1,500 and 1,800 miles in his head. By the time he was released, his imaginary voyage had taken him 31,936 kilometers—almost twenty-thousand miles.[42]

On the scheduled day of his release, a crowd of journalists assembled before the prison, at midnight on October 1, 1966. Prisoner Number Five was by then sixty-one years old, and it was a graying man who walked through the prison gates into the blinding barrage of projectors and flashes. Despite his age and his years of incarceration, he retained something of his former elegance.

The only member of his family who came to meet him was his wife. He greeted her with a cool embrace and these words: "My sentence was just," before getting into her car. He shared his first impressions as a free man with the German newspaper, *Der Spiegel.*

A family reunion was planned the next day in a hunting lodge on Lake Kellersee in northern Germany, where fifteen or so of his closest relations gathered to greet him after so many years. But the party turned sour. As welcoming and natural as everyone tried to be, their attempts at conversation failed. His adult children no longer knew who he was, while their spouses, who had never met him, tried vainly to develop a rapport with him and ease the tension. No one succeeded in finding the right words. As soon as Speer turned the conversation to his life in Spandau—a refrain well-known to everyone already—it only made matters worse. His children wanted to talk about their lives, their projects, their ideas, their friends; he only wanted to talk about himself. His wife thought "it was probably too much to ask of him."[43] Two worlds faced off in silence that first day: the future and the past, freedom and prison. His daughter Margret remembered that it was also out of the question to talk about life before Spandau, which left the family spinning its wheels with hardly anything to talk about.[44] Speer's wife was equally reticent to speak of the past : "Enough about those old stories!" was invariably her answer to questions about the war and National Socialism.[45]

It was clear to everyone: no communication would ever be possible with their father and husband. In 1978, when Gitta Sereny interviewed him in Heidelberg, he blamed himself for his failure to communicate with his family, saying he never knew how to go about it. His presence weighed on the family. Like most parents, he took pleasure in following his children's success in school and later at university. He was particularly interested in Albert's architecture studies since they shared the same career choice. At Spandau, he had wondered if their tense relations would continue after he came home; the disastrous family reunion seemed to indicate they would, and the conclusion was a bitter pill to swallow. Even at Spandau, he had never felt so alone. He began to miss his spartan life in prison, his books, and his imaginary walks, but he realized nothing would ever be the same. His children were of the same mind. Hilde recalled that—one by one—they stopped trying, in the absence of any point of connection between them. Albert Jr. would remember: "My father admired my work as an architect, but he didn't understand it. We were coming from two different worlds."[46] His children began to plan their visits to their mother in Heidelberg around their father's absences, but Speer did not seem bothered by this: his sole concern was restoring his reputation. He received requests for interviews from around the world, and the house in Heidelberg saw a steady flow of visitors.

In 1971, in an interview he granted to Eric Norden for *Playboy*, Speer recognized his tacit approval of the mass killings, explaining that, "I saw nothing because I didn't want to see anything."[47] In the article, the journalist does not hide the unease he felt during the interview, listening to an impassive Speer accuse himself of terrible crimes and then offer the journalist a piece of apple pie without missing a beat.[48] Some years later, Speer admitted to Gitta Sereny: "I sensed . . . that dreadful things were happening with the Jews."[49]

His books were enormous successes. *Inside the Third Reich* provided a unique perspective by a high-ranking Nazi official. *Inside the Walls of Spandau* is a collection of more than twenty thousand notes Speer recorded in prison using any paper at hand, including toilet paper, which he found particularly invaluable for his purposes.[50] *Inside the Third Reich* sold more than two hundred thousand copies in Germany and became a bestseller in the United States.

In his last years, Speer lived quietly in his house in the Allgäu. His marriage had withered, and he had taken a mistress, which did nothing to improve his relations with his children. He received fewer and fewer visitors but he did accept to be interviewed by Matthias Schmidt, who was writing his doctoral thesis on National Socialism. Speer put him in contact with his old friend, Rudolf Wolters, but Wolters had not approved of the way Speer had moved the blame for his actions onto Hitler, nor did he appreciate the fact that Speer never mentioned him in his books. Wolters provided Schmidt with the draft of his own *Chronicles*, in which Wolters reported on Speer's activities between 1941 and 1945, arguing that Speer was actively involved in the Reich's worst crimes. He included documents, signed by Speer, ordering the removal of Jews from Berlin. All of it was proof of Speer's deliberate misleading of the court at Nuremberg.

Speer died in 1981 from a heart attack in a hotel in London where he had traveled—accompanied by his mistress—to record an interview for the BBC with Henry T. King Jr., one of the American prosecutors at Nuremberg, and Norman Stone, a professor of history at Oxford.

Some of Speer's children maintain they have suppressed any memory of Adolf Hitler; they cannot allow themselves to admit they were in such close contact with a man who, Hilde Speer says, "revolts" her. As for photos showing her holding Hitler's hand, dressed in a little white skirt with flowers in her hair, she says she does not remember the incident. Or, perhaps she chooses not to, as a way of leaving the past behind. It is impossible to say which.

Hilde Schramm became a sociologist and has been active in politics. She was the leader of the Green Party in Germany and became vice president of the Berlin city council. In 2004, she was awarded the Moses Mendelssohn Award for her work promoting interfaith tolerance and reconciliation. The award ceremony was scheduled to take place in a synagogue in Berlin but had to be moved to a Catholic church, under pressure from the Jewish community, despite the support of Albert Meyer, the community's spokesperson. It was inconceivable that the daughter of Albert Speer, one of the war's principal criminals, could receive such a distinction in a Jewish temple.

Hilde Schramm understood their objections and respected their decision.[51]

The Nazis systematically impounded the property of Europe's Jews, which was then shipped to Germany and sold at auction. Hilde Schramm has made a point of asking Germans to question where their own property and artwork, even their jobs, came from and how they were obtained, paying particular attention to the years between 1933 and 1945. "We who survived the war are not guilty," she told *The Guardian* in 2005. "We did not inherit the guilt, but the consequences of the wrong-doing of the past. To that we have to try and act with responsibility."[52] By that she means returning wrongfully acquired property to its rightful owners.

Hilde initially refused accepting the paintings that she inherited from her father, because he had purchased them at very advantageous prices from Jews, who were probably forced to sell them. She changed her mind, however, when an opportunity arose to turn them into good: she sold them and donated the profits, which came to seventy thousand pounds, to the foundation she created, *Zurückgeben* (Give Back), which supports Jewish women working in the arts and sciences.[53] She explained in that same interview that she thinks guilt does not accurately express her feelings, but rather shame: "I've reached the conclusion that you can only be guilty of things you've done yourself, or not done, for that matter. . . . I feel ashamed of what happened in the past, and of course I feel ashamed that it happened so close to me, in my own family. For that I still feel shame."[54] Speer saw clearly that his legacy would always be his children's biggest challenge in life.[55] Like her siblings, Hilde declines to speak anymore of her father, to avoid further questions by the press and to focus on the present. She would rather not be associated any longer with a man whose legacy is an embarrassment, but the politician she is knows that if his story can turn attention to her foundation, she will take it. She is clear-eyed about her situation and thinks the time has come to write her own biography.[56]

Margret, the youngest daughter, is a photographer and the mother of four children. She married young and has been living under her husband's name, Nissen, for many years. In her book, *Sind Sie die Tochter Speer?* (*Are You Speer's Daughter?*), she describes what it was like to live in the shadow of Hitler's architect.[57] The title was inspired by a question one of her colleagues asked her—point-blank—upon learning her maiden name. At the time, she was working as a photographer in Berlin, as part of an exposition, "The Topography of Terror," and recognized herself in one of the photos: a smiling little girl, standing confidently next to Hitler. Margret wonders how her father could have placed his skills in the service of the Nazi regime. She describes Speer in his many manifestations: father, architect, Nazi, prisoner, writer. She resents this man who abandoned his family and left his devoted wife for a mistress. She is uncomfortable admitting she is Speer's daughter, but she wants to preserve her memories and refuses to feel any guilt. As a girl, she could never believe her father was a criminal, since he had never committed a murder himself. Later, she could not accept the scope of his involvement in the activities of the Reich. Her denial is similar to Speer's, when, in reference to the genocide of the Jews, he confessed in the *Playboy* interview that he chose to look the other way. She explains her father's choices by his opportunism and his ruthless ambition.

She also describes a man wholly absorbed by his work and

driven to create an oeuvre that would outlast the context in which it was created. Her analysis is echoed by Speer: "I felt myself to be Hitler's architect. Political events did not concern me. My job was merely to provide impressive backdrops for such events."[58]

During his final years, Speer was preoccupied by his reputation, to the detriment of his relationships with his children. Yet they would spend their lives asking themselves about him, whose name the sons at least continue to bear. They were never able to confront him personally about his actions; he may have accepted responsibility for these but he always denied any knowledge of the Nazis' crimes.

Other Nazi children did have the opportunity to confront their fathers. One was the son of Josef Mengele, even though this Nazi criminal never regretted what he did.

ROLF MENGELE

The Son of "The Angel of Death"

Sale 45 held on July 21, 2011, at Alexander Autographs, an auctioneer specializing in historical autographs and militia in Stamford, Connecticut, included a one-of-a-kind item, a collection of journals, whose historic value was summed up as follows: "Taken as a whole and carefully read and analyzed, this archive, the vast majority of which has never been published or perhaps even viewed, offers an in-depth view into the cruelest mind of the twentieth century."[1] The expected sale price of Lot 4? Between three hundred thousand and four hundred thousand dollars.

Sold! The auctioneer's hammer falls. The winning bid has been phoned in to the sale, and these 3,380 pages, handwritten in blue ink, now belong to an ultra-Orthodox Jew and son of a Holocaust survivor for the sum of $245,000. The buyer, who wishes to remain anonymous, intends to make these journals accessible to the public, to discredit negationist arguments, and to warn against any form of doctrine that could lead to discrimination.

The lot consists of thirty-one spiral school notebooks, with variously colored covers—black, khaki, green, and checkered—marked, in Spanish, *Cuaderno* (notebook), *Cultura General* or *Agenda Classica*. The pages are covered with uniform, angular handwriting that leans to the right. Drawings and sketches are interspersed with autobiographical anecdotes, poems, and philosophical and political musings. The entries date from 1960 to 1975.

The sale caused a stir: some observers objected to a commercial value being placed on documents such as these; others denounced the entire transaction as simply obscene.

The journals' author writes under a pseudonym, Andreas, and speaks of himself in the third person: precautions taken by one of the most wanted criminals of the twentieth century to remain anonymous and undiscovered. He describes how he traveled through a Europe devastated by war—all the way to South America—and then traveled more, through Argentina, Paraguay, and Brazil. He provides details about the experiments he conducted and their contributions (in his opinion) to humanity. The author is still committed to the ideology of National Socialism and he explains his theories concerning overpopulation, eugenics, and euthanasia.

"When you start mixing the races, civilization declines," he writes in the diary he kept between 1960 and 1962.[2] "There's no 'good' or 'bad' in nature. There's only 'appropriate' or 'inappropriate' . . . Things that are 'inappropriate' fall through since they lose in the struggle for survival. . . . Biology doesn't support equal rights. Women shouldn't be working in higher positions. Women's work must depend on filling a biological quota. Birth control can be done by sterilizing those with deficient genes. Those with good genes will be sterilized after the fifth child."[3]

The notebooks were discovered in 2004 in São Paulo in the home of a couple who had lodged the author of these lines. They were returned to his only biological son, who may or may not be the person who sold them through a third party to Alexander Autographs.

Bent with age, Josef Mengele sits every day at his writing table, reliving his glory days and his interminable journey to escape capture. Fifteen years separate his departure from Germany and his first journal entries, but his convictions have never wavered during the thirty-four years he has spent on the run. Convinced of his innocence, he has become a compulsive writer in exile, and he spends most of his time in his home on the outskirts of São Paulo hunched over his notebooks, which he also fills with drawings of Bavarian-style furniture, houses, animals, and plants. His other activities are gardening, woodworking, and walking.

The year is 1977, and he is anxiously waiting to be reunited with his son, Rolf; they have not seen each other for twenty-one years. That was in 1956, and Rolf did not even recognize his father then, who was introduced to the boy under an assumed identity. This time, his son will know him, Josef Mengele, one of the most wanted Nazis in the world, the one who earned the nickname "The Angel of Death" because of the macabre experiments he conducted at Auschwitz.

It has taken five years to prepare Rolf's visit without tipping off the Nazi hunters who are always on the lookout for him. Josef's lawyer, Hans Sedlmeier, first met with Rolf in Germany, and then arranged a meeting between Rolf and his cousin, Karl-Heinz, who had lived several years with Josef in Argentina. Hans Sedlmeier wanted to make sure that Rolf understood that people of his father's generation who had lived during the war could have vastly different analyses of the Third Reich than those of the newer generation of Germans who only read about the period in history books. He also needed to send money to his client via Rolf. The Sedlmeiers have always been staunch supporters of Josef Mengele.

Following his father's advice, Rolf would be travelling to Brazil using the passport of a friend, which he had managed to purloin while the two were on vacation together. Nothing could stop him from seeing his father again, even though the old man is no longer his childhood hero. In fact, Rolf is sure they have nothing in common, a sentiment he would later explain as follows: "On the contrary, my opinions were diametrically opposed. I didn't even bother to listen to him or think of his ideas. I simply rejected everything that he presented. My personal attitude to national and international politics was never in doubt. My liberal political views, partly even 'to the left,' were known. As a result of my many critical remarks, sometimes I was even suspected of being a communist."[4]

When night falls and he hears the old bus come down the dusty street outside his window, Josef starts, and begins to tremble. He waits, willing himself motionless, with his bony hands clenched into fists in his pants pockets, his face like a mask. He who always took such care with his appearance is oblivious to what he looks like tonight: tonight, his son is arriving, and with him, perhaps, Nazi hunters. The obsessive fear of being captured always haunts him, even at this point in his miserable life. He is a man eaten by anxiety, a mere shadow of the cold and calculating doctor who reigned at Auschwitz. He has nervous ticks now: he sucks on his mustache continuously, so that he has hairballs in his guts like a cat. These disrupt his digestion and cause him terrible pain, even threaten his life. Still, he can never let his guard down.

Josef has lived alone for years. His yellow stucco house has a pointed roof and white windows and sits on a wooded lot, so that it reminds him of an alpine chalet. Its only furnishings are a table, some chairs, a bed, and an armoire.

When he sees his son enter the yard through the wooden gate, Josef is overcome with emotion. Tears flood his eyes and he feels weak at the knees but he manages to greet him on the front steps, this son who has dared to come all the way to Brazil to see him. He tells Rolf that he thinks of him as a brave soldier, whose courage has taken him across enemy lines.[5] But this was not always the case.

Today however, Rolf is Josef's hero. He has taken numerous risks to meet the man who never bothered much to know him. When Rolf was a child, his father was too busy with his deadly work for the Nazis. By the time Rolf was an adolescent, his father was on the run from the Allies and Nazi hunters both. Letters were their only means of communication, and a superficial one at that.

It was Rolf's wish to see this father he barely knew, in the flesh, face-to-face. He has only ever seen him on two other occasions. Nevertheless, he is surprised to find that the master of disguise who has eluded capture for so long is a frail old man, ravaged by time. He knows how important this meeting is to his father. As for himself, he has not come all this way at great risk to prosecute the Allies' most wanted criminal, but rather to try to understand how this man, his own father, could have actively participated in the vast Nazi death machine.

Rolf is an attorney practicing law in Fribourg, Germany. In his family's opinion, he is a radical leftist, the clan's black sheep. For his part, he refuses to see any similarities between himself and the Mengeles except for the bloodline they share through his father, the most hated man in the world. Rolf is thirty-three, the same age as his father when he was the camp doctor at Auschwitz, deciding the fates of millions of people with the wave of a hand.

Survivors of the camp never forgot the Mediterranean-looking man in an impeccable uniform and spit-shined boots, who always carried a horsewhip and who selected the victims of his experiments with a gesture of a single finger. If he pointed to the right, you lived but were sent to his hospital. If he pointed to the left, you died. He never showed any emotion as he sent men, women, children, and infants either to the gas chambers or to his somber experiments, humming an opera by Wagner or Puccini all the while. He was the central cog of the death machine.

Rolf can only manage a weak, "Hello, Father." The two men exchange a brief, stiff embrace, as is their nature; neither is used to showing much emotion. Rolf has decided he will be polite no matter what, telling himself: "When all is said and done, he is still my father." Still, he does not soften to him until he feels his father's tears running down his cheeks.

This is their second meeting since Josef fled Europe. It will also be their last. When they first met, Rolf's mother introduced Josef to him as his "Uncle Fritz" who lived in South America. Much later, he would discover that his so-called uncle was in fact his father and he would learn of the role his father played in Germany's darkest years. Seeing him now, Rolf is torn between filial piety and an instinctive rejection of this man who was capable of such barbarity. The rest of the world may label him a war criminal, but for the Mengele family, he is still an honorable and brilliant doctor. They are a family of wealthy industrialists from Bavaria composed of three sons, Josef being the eldest; their sole concern is keeping the family name out of the mud.

The family business was manufacturing farm machinery, and the factory was one of the largest employers in the Bavarian city of Günzburg. The family astutely parlayed its support of National Socialism into becoming the third largest company in its sector under the Third Reich. Hitler himself gave a speech at "Karl Mengele & Söhne." The firm still operates today and its headquarters in the city center still proudly bears the family name. There is even a Karl Mengele street, named after Josef's father. But of Günzburg's most infamous son, all traces have been erased.

Young Josef never gravitated toward the family business and passed on his right of succession to his younger brothers. He was a top student with an insatiable ambition who saw his future elsewhere, preferably in the history books.

In 1930, when he began studying philosophy, anthropology, and medicine in Munich, Nazi ideals had already infiltrated German universities. Some of Mengele's earliest professors were staunch eugenicists such as Ernst Rüdin, who pioneered the German law of forced sterilization of individuals with hereditary defects. Five years later, in 1935, he defended his doctoral thesis entitled "Morphological Research on the Lower Jaw Section of Four Racial Groups" under the direction of Theodor Mollison, a specialist in "racial hygiene" at the University of Munich. Josef Mengele was already persuaded of the existence of a superior Germanic, Aryan-type race, and he set out to prove it through science.

He became an assistant to Otmar von Verschuer who was a prominent eugenicist and director of the Institute for Hereditary Biology and Racial Hygiene in Frankfurt, whose theories led to National Socialism's interest in genetics. Von Verschuer was convinced that twins held the genes for a blond, blue-eyed Aryan race. Under his direction, Mengele earned a second diploma from the University of Frankfurt in 1938, but not before joining the National Socialist party in 1937 as member 5574974. Upon graduating, he joined the SS, swearing for the "purity" of his own racial background, which he claimed to trace back to 1744.

Mengele believed that genetic manipulation was the key to Germany's future. By studying twins, he hoped to create a German race that would multiply and grow the German nation.[6] With his mentor, Von Verschuer, he sought to identify the genes thought to be responsible for a pure, Aryan race. The National Socialist party was keen to back up its theories about racial hygiene with science, and Mengele contributed his research to the cause.

Before Mengele would agree to marry Irene Schoenbein in 1939, she first had to satisfy him that her paternal lineage was free of Jewish ancestry. No proof; no wedding. She succeeded by emphasizing her "Nordic side," and the union was declared acceptable. This tall blonde was the love of Mengele's life, and she was both very devoted to him and very jealous. They would never enjoy a normal life as husband and wife, however. Mengele was singularly driven by professional ambition and patriotism, committing Irene to a life of solitude. Only two months after the wedding—at the moment of Germany's invasion of Poland—Mengele enlisted in the German army, leaving his young bride behind without an afterthought.

He joined the medical corps of the SS Wiking Division, which was dispatched to the Eastern front and to Ukraine in particular. Mengele was awarded the Iron Cross for saving and treating two German soldiers, but, injured in combat, he returned to Berlin in 1942 where he took up his genetics research with his former mentor. Von Verschuer had been appointed to lead the Kaiser Wilhelm Institute, a scientific research body that advanced Nazi theories on eugenics and racial hygiene from 1927 to 1945.

Six months later in late May 1943, Mengele—who in April had been promoted to the rank of Hauptsturmführer—was assigned to Auschwitz, the largest concentration camp built by the Nazis, forty miles west of Kraków near the Polish border with Czechoslovakia.

Auschwitz was an implacable machine of industrialized killing. Smoke belched day and night from its four complexes containing the gas chambers and crematoriums; the smell of burning human flesh hung in the unbreathable air, a stink that was even worse in the warm months. The camp was enormous, consisting of three main sections that were constantly being expanded; identical redbrick and wood barracks stretched as far as the eye could see. Mengele was probably unperturbed by the sight when he arrived there and reported to barrack number ten.

His priority was to get to work as quickly as possible. He viewed Auschwitz and its unlimited potential for experimentation on "human guinea pigs" as a unique opportunity for the advancement of both science and his racial theories. He sent human samples, marked with the label "Urgent: War

Materials," regularly to his colleagues at the Kaiser Wilhelm Institute to analyze.

When Mengele was in school, his classmates teased him as being "the gypsy"[7] because of his swarthy looks, black hair, and hazel eyes, and he later joked that he more closely resembled a gypsy than an Aryan. Yet he sent over fifteen hundred Romas to their deaths only a few days after he began at Auschwitz.

Irene did not move to the camp with her husband but chose to stay in Germany. Mengele spent eighteen months at Auschwitz; Irene visited him there on only two occasions, in August 1943, and again in August 1944, a few months after the birth of Rolf, who did not accompany her on the trip. When she questioned her husband about the cause of the infernal smell at the camp, she was told to never again ask him about it.[8] Nevertheless, Irene's subsequent visit to the camp was like a second honeymoon for Mengele's wife—an idyllic moment with the man she loved. In her diaries, she noted nothing about her husband's activities or the functioning of the camp, only that she swam in the Sola river, picked blueberries, and made jam.[9] Mengele was a cold and cynical man who kept his secrets to himself and avoided interacting with his colleagues. He took pride in his rank and his war decorations, particularly his Iron Cross, which he wore constantly. He kept apart from everyone to better concentrate on what he believed was his destined calling: to further the evolution of mankind, never mind that his methods were anything but humane or compassionate.

Mengele intrigued several of his colleagues at Auschwitz, among them Hans Münch, who remarked about the Auschwitz doctor: "He was an ideologue, body and soul. . . . Never any emotion; he showed no hate or fanaticism. And in this way he saw the gassings as the only rational solution, and as the Jews were going to die anyway, he saw no reason not to use them first for medical experiments."[10] To his colleagues, Dr. Mengele was a mystery, whose discretion and reserve discouraged any familiarity. He told no one of Rolf's birth in 1944, and did not travel to be at his wife's side for the event.

Little Rolf lived alone with his mother in Freiburg im Breisgau in the Black Forest. Josef came to meet his son for the first time in November 1944 when the baby was eight months old. In April 1945, mother and son moved to Autenried in Bavaria to be closer to Josef's family. Rolf grew up with his grandparents and finally knew the pleasures of family life.

At Auschwitz, trains arrived at all hours from all over Europe. Newcomers went through a first round of selection—to separate those deemed capable of forced labor—from the rest who were sent straight to the gas chambers, which were made to look like showers. Mengele was present to see every new trainload arrive, his eyes on the lookout for twins whom he needed for his sinister experiments. These usually ended in death for the victims after horrible suffering. He was hoping to understand the inheritance mechanisms of genes and to eradicate so-called weak genes. Nothing made his face light up like the news that twins had arrived in camp.

His countless experiments were administered without anesthesia: blood and bone marrow transfusions, injections of infectious diseases, amputation of limbs, organ removal, sterilization. Mengele was also interested in eye color and the possibility of changing it, injecting chemicals into the eyes of his "patients" who usually went blind following these experiments. His objective was the creation of a superior race that would satisfy the ideals of National Socialism.

When Mengele fled Auschwitz on January 17, 1945, he left mountains of cadavers behind him. Few of his "human guinea pigs" survived his macabre experiments, even though they were granted a momentary stay of execution to participate in his studies. As the Reich fell, the westward stream of German soldiers provided Mengele the cover he needed to escape the Allies. He traded his SS uniform for a Wehrmacht uniform and lay low in Czechoslovakia. Overwhelmed by the numbers of fleeing soldiers, the Allies ordered the arrest of SS members only: these men had their blood type tattooed onto the underside of the left arm, making them easily identifiable. Mengele was very protective of his body, however, and had refused to be tattooed. Irene would explain to Rolf that his father was so particular about his appearance that he considered a tattoo an unthinkable violation of his person, both unsightly and repulsive[11] for a man who prided himself on his tailor-made suits and spent hours gazing at himself in the mirror and admiring the softness of his skin. In the absence of a comprehensive list of war criminals established by the Allies, his vanity saved him.

Irene remained without news of Josef for a short time after the war ended until the wife of one of his doctor friends informed her that he was still alive. His name had begun to circulate, however, and the Allies were on the lookout for any information that would lead them to him. The Mengele family was placed under surveillance and interrogated but they revealed nothing. The German newspaper *Bund* reported that the family feared the possibility that they could be sued for reparations by Josef's victims.

When Irene was questioned by two American officers, she told them he had disappeared and had likely died on the Eastern Front. She had taken pains to create the illusion of this fiction by dressing in widow's weeds and arranging for a funeral mass to be said for her husband at the church in Günzburg.[12] Irene may have turned a blind eye to Mengele's activities while he was at Auschwitz, but she could not have remained ignorant after the war, and yet she chose not to denounce him.

After a brief stop in Munich, Mengele returned to his ancestral grounds, hiding in the forests outside Günzburg, where his family regularly made food drops for him. The authorities noticed nothing unusual; a report filed by the Israeli police made no mention of any contact between Mengele and his family.

In late 1945, the "Angel of Death" was living under the assumed name of Fritz Hollman and working as a farmhand in Rosenheim, in Bavaria. Masquerading as Rolf's uncle living in South America, Mengele would use the same name to meet his son years later. Mengele's family often visited him in Rosenheim; Irene came frequently, meeting her husband discreetly at a lake, and sometimes brought two-year-old Rolf. A photo taken during one of these visits shows a smiling Josef behind Rolf. On most occasions, however, Irene came alone. In November 1946, Mengele visited his wife and son in Autenried for two weeks, believing the Allies had suspended their manhunt.

Rolf would remember the four years that followed the war as an unhappy and anxious time for his mother. Her one wish was to lead a traditional life as wife and mother within a close-knit family; instead, she found herself married to a fugitive with whom she had never shared a home and who was becoming a complete stranger to her. The Mengeles' marriage, already weakened by the war, had little strength to resist its present trials. Irene, who had suffered for years from the strain of her solitary existence, could no longer ignore that her husband was no longer the man she had married. She sought out the company of other men, no matter that it sent Josef into a blind rage. Pathologically jealous, he berated his wife every time she left the house, resulting in spectacular arguments. For some years already, Irene was herself a changed woman, no longer Josef's devoted wife as she had been in the early years of their marriage. She recognized that as long as she stayed with Mengele, she would live a fugitive's life. In 1948, during one of her absences from the house that so infuriated Mengele, she met the man who would become her second husband: Alfons Hackenjos, the owner of a shoe store in Freiburg im Breisgau. Little Rolf, who was four years old, would come to think of him as the first father figure he had ever known.

When he learned that his name had been cited in the "Doctors' Trial" that was held at Nuremberg beginning in December 1946 following the trials of the major war criminals, Mengele, who had let his guard down for some time, realized the noose was tightening around him. He decided to flee to South America and boarded the *North King* in the port of Genoa, Italy, in the summer of 1949, carrying a false passport bearing the name of Helmut Gregor. He was still hopeful that Irene and Rolf would join him in Buenos Aires as soon as he could send for them, but it was never to be. Irene could not bear to leave Germany or her family and refused to live a fugitive's life on the other side of the world. Her main reason, however, was that she had a new man in her life, and while she still had some feelings for Rolf's father, she did not intend to give up her new relationship.

In 1954, Irene, in love with Alfons and tired of her situation, asked Josef for a divorce. Rolf never had any reason to believe that his father's activities at Auschwitz played into her decision to leave the marriage since the couple adhered to a simple rule: "Don't ask, don't tell."[13] Irene was happy to finally part ways with her in-laws, and even happier that she needed no financial help from them. That same year, Mengele decided to abandon his assumed identity and live under his real name, making the change official at the West German embassy. The divorce was pronounced on March 25, 1954, and delivered to Josef Mengele. The "Angel of Death" had risen from the dead.

He returned to Europe in 1956, meeting Rolf again during a family vacation in Switzerland. The boy was then twelve but still knew him only as his Uncle Fritz from South America. Martha, the pretty widow of Josef's brother, and her son, Karl-Heinz, were also there on holiday. Every morning, Rolf and his cousin climbed into Uncle Fritz's bed to listen to his grand stories of battles he had fought on the Russian front. Rolf remembered the vacation as the best he had ever known: no one treated him like a little boy anymore and he was happy, despite his intensifying rivalry with Karl-Heinz on whom Fritz doted, at Rolf's expense. He did not know that his so-called uncle was having an affair with his real aunt Martha.

Two years later, in 1958, Mengele married his sister-in-law in Montevideo, Uruguay. Martha and Karl-Heinz moved to Argentina for several years.

Mengele blended in easily in Juan Perón's Buenos Aires. Argentina had become the Eldorado of Nazis on the run and would remain so until Perón's death. When many of these Nazis moved on to Paraguay, Mengele followed. As for Martha and Karl-Heinz, they preferred to return to Germany. Contrary to rumor, Mengele stayed only two years in Paraguay before moving to Brazil in 1962. During all this time, and even though he returned to Germany twice—in 1956 and 1959, under his true identity—he was never arrested. It was also during these years that Irene decided to explain to Rolf the reasons for his father's absence: he had either died or disappeared on the Russian front, but in either case he was a hero. For over ten years, Rolf believed his father was dead, all the while exchanging long letters with Uncle Fritz, whom he never dreamt for a moment was his father, alive and well.

Rolf was sixteen when he learned that the uncle who had joined them on holiday in Switzerland three years earlier was his biological father, Josef Mengele. Rolf recalled how the news hit him: "My father was always the war hero who died on the Eastern Front. He was cultivated and spoke Greek and Latin. The truth was a shock to me. It wasn't at all good news to discover I was the son of Josef Mengele."[14] At school, he was taunted by his classmates who teased him as the son of a war criminal and called him a "little Nazi" or "SS Mengele." Rolf responded with irony: "Oh yes, and I'm also Adolf Eichmann's nephew." His teachers attributed his laziness to the trauma caused by his absent father, who was alternately a hero and an executioner.

Mengele's attempts to develop an affectionate father-son relationship with Rolf were unsuccessful. The letters he wrote to Rolf were cold and distant, as if he were trying to replicate the relationship he had had with his own father. Mengele even wrote and illustrated a children's book for Rolf but his efforts were in vain. Rolf was particularly resentful of his father's affection and esteem for his cousin, Karl-Heinz. In reality, Mengele was much closer to his nephew and stepson, with whom he had an almost paternal relationship, while for Rolf he would remain forever a stranger. This was the reason Rolf needed to confront him, face-to-face, this reclusive, depressed, and suicidal old man that Josef Mengele had become, a far cry from the hero that his mother had invented for him.

Mengele's lodgings in São Paulo are spartan; he invites his son to take his own bed, explaining he will sleep on a mattress on the floor. They will have no need, however: Rolf wants answers, and they talk late into the night. At first, Rolf avoids the question of his father's involvement at Auschwitz but when he finally questions Josef, the frail, elderly man reacts immediately: "How could you believe I ever did those things? Can't you see those were lies, propaganda?" He defends himself virulently: "I didn't dream up Auschwitz and I'm not personally responsible for what happened there. Auschwitz existed long before me. I wanted to help, but my influence was very limited. I couldn't help everyone."

When Rolf asks him how the subjects of his experiments were chosen from among the new arrivals, Mengele admits he participated. "What was I supposed to do with these people? They were sick and half-dead when they arrived. You can't imagine the conditions there." He wants Rolf to know that his job was *only* to determine who was fit to work and that he did his best to see that as many of the new arrivals as possible were given that designation. By his count, he guesses he saved the lives of several thousand people. He wasn't the one who ordered the exterminations; he cannot be held responsible for that. He swears he never killed or hurt anyone personally.

Rolf sees things differently, however: "It's impossible for anyone who was at Auschwitz not to have tried every day to leave that place. It is impossible and horrible both to not have tried. I will never understand how human beings could do those things. That my father was one of them doesn't change my opinion. For me, what happened is entirely unethical and immoral and is an affront to our understanding of human nature." His late-night discussions with his father convince him that Josef regrets nothing and is still a National Socialist sympathizer who believes in the superiority of the Aryan race, a theory that Mengele supports by drawing on sociological, historical, and political arguments. Rolf listens but notes that his ideas are, paradoxically, hardly scientific at all.[15] Mengele concludes that he only did his duty and obeyed the rules in order to survive. For those reasons, he absolves himself of all guilt. Rolf understands that Josef refuses to be the monster that he is in the eyes of the rest of the world.

Rolf asks him another question: if he is so convinced that he acted justly, why doesn't he surrender to the authorities to be judged? Mengele answers him tersely: "There are no judges, only avengers."[16]

Rolf never senses an ounce of humanity, compassion, or regret in his father. He leaves him at the end of two weeks knowing he will never see him again. As for Mengele, he feels he can finally die in peace. Perhaps he felt the need to justify himself to his sole descendent, to prove he was not the monster his son believed he was, but a man who simply followed orders.

Nevertheless, Rolf never turned Josef in. The reason he gives: it was impossible for him to betray his father. Unlike Niklas Frank, who detested his father, Hans Frank, Rolf's feeling was that he never knew his father well enough to hate him.

Two years after that meeting, in 1979, Rolf received a letter from friends of his father in Brazil: "Our friend left us on a tropical beach." Josef Mengele had died of a heart attack while swimming in the ocean, after thirty-four years of surviving on the run. The Mengele family decided against announcing the news in order to elude the question of their own complicity in helping him avoid being brought to justice.

Nine months later, Rolf returned to Brazil to put his father's affairs in order and recover his personal effects, traveling under his true identity. On his way back to Europe, he checked into the same hotel in Rio de Janeiro where he had stayed during his previous trip under an assumed identity. This time, the concierge commented on his name: "Ah, Mengele. Do you know you have a very famous name around here?"[17] Terrified, Rolf hurried to his room to hide his father's last possessions in the room's dropped ceiling, even though he was sure they would be easily found there if the police ever ordered a search. He had recovered from his father's belongings a gold watch, some letters, and his diaries. The authorities would never come looking for him however, and those same diaries would be offered for sale at the much decried auction that took place in 2011.

In the meantime, Rolf kept a close eye on the hotel's guests and tried to make himself invisible in case the concierge thought to alert the police. Even with Josef dead, the Mengeles had to keep their secret safe. Rolf justified his silence on the need to protect those who had helped his father over the years and on the absence of any evidence of his death.

The news of Josef Mengele's death finally broke six years later. His friends and sympathizers had known all along, but they never violated their unwritten code of silence. It was during a police raid of the home of Mengele's confidence man, Hans Sedlmeier, in 1985 that correspondence between the two men was discovered, including a condolence card sent by Mengele's friends in Brazil.

Josef's nephew, Dieter Mengele, saw no other choice—as the president of the family business—to announce the news of his uncle's death and to submit to an interview with the press. His concern was to head off any possible repercussions on the family business, if the extent of the family's help to Josef were to become known. Dieter denied the family had provided any financial assistance or even maintained any correspondence with him. Rolf was never consulted on the family's decision, a fact for which he would reproach his cousin. As for proof of Mengele's death, the body was ordered exhumed; however, on the day of the exhumation, the only person who could make a positive identification was unreachable. That was Rolf, who happened to be on vacation, and who only learned upon his return what the rest of the world by that time already knew when he turned on the television at home.

Over the thirty years and more that Mengele lived in hiding, there were often rumors that he had been spotted in such and such a place. Even the Israeli Secret Service declared it had "periodically picked up his trace, while never succeeding in apprehending him."[18] Nevertheless, and in spite of his obsessive fears of being arrested or abducted by the Mossad or by Nazi hunters, he did not hesitate to travel back to Europe and live under his true identity. He was buried, however, under a false name, Wolfgang Gehrard, at Embu near São Paulo. Following the exhumation on June 6, 1985, carried out by the Brazilian police at the request of the German government, an analysis of the jawbone was sufficient to identify the body, but a DNA test would not confirm those results until 1992. The delay was caused by Rolf, who refused to provide a blood sample that would allow a match to be made.[19]

With so many international organizations and Nazi hunters looking for him, it defies reason that Mengele eluded the authorities for over thirty-four years. In 1960, the Mossad located both Eichmann, the man who designed the Final Solution, and Mengele, but had to choose which one to capture; Auschwitz's infamous doctor narrowly escaped arrest on that occasion, but how did he succeed so many times before and after?

Rolf went public with his story in 1985, describing his meeting with his father and revealing some of Mengele's writings. The family definitively cut off all relations with him from that moment forward.

Unlike certain other Nazi children, Rolf is unconvinced that barbarity can be contained in a gene that can be handed down through the generations. He decided to change his name, however, to close the book on his past and in the interests of his own descendants. In the 1980s, he adopted his wife's name and settled in Munich working as an attorney.

He believes his children have the right to live free of their grandfather's crimes. He owes them both the truth and that freedom. He thinks that the only lesson to be learned from his family is to know to distinguish good from evil and to reflect on what is important in life. His destiny was to become the son of Josef Mengele and to bear the struggles of that inheritance. He wanted to get into politics but certain people, whether Jewish businessmen or victims of the war, refused to work with him, although he will never know their reasons.

In 2008, he wrote to an Israeli newspaper, asking the Jewish people not to hate him. He wanted to travel to Israel and visit the Yad Vashem Holocaust memorial, but, he wrote, "I am afraid that the survivors of the Shoah and their descendants will be upset if they learn who I am."[20]

Rolf Mengele is the only Nazi child examined in this book who for many years did not even know he was the child of a Nazi official and who was able to question his father later about his role in the Nazi death machine. Yet their discussions were fruitless in the sense that Mengele never stopped believing in the Nazi ideals, never assumed any responsibility for what he did, and even argued that he had helped save lives. Rolf felt he could never betray his father, however, and never wanted to, even after his father's death and even despite his own conviction that his children should never have to live under the weight of the name of Mengele.

CONCLUSION

A German Story?

A muffled thud rumbles through the auditorium at the annual convention of the Christian Democratic Union of the Federal Republic of Germany in Berlin. Amplified by a microphone, it is the sound of a hand delivering a vigorous slap across the face.

It is a woman's hand and it was aimed at someone who, like many Germans, thought he could cover up his involvement with the Nazis. But this man, Kurt Georg Kiesinger, is the German chancellor, and the slap is one way of throwing his past in his face. Up until this moment, evidently, that past has not concerned his fellow Germans, who elected him to the chancellery. In 1968, however, times are changing. Not only are the taboos and rigid morals of the Nazi era disintegrating, the far-left terrorist group known as the Red Army Faction is forming in a climate of spreading social unrest.

By the late 1940s, a majority of West Germans had wanted to turn the page on the war and put an end to the denazification trials, which many resented as both a burden imposed by the Allies and an obstacle to the country's democratization. Responding to those demands while hoping to curry favor, then Chancellor Konrad Adenauer ended the trials and instituted a rehabilitation program for certain Nazis who were not known criminals: a policy that would allow many Nazi officials to avoid indictment and arrest. Josef Mengele's visit to Germany was a perfect example, but he was not the only criminal who eluded justice.

The hand that slapped the chancellor belonged to Beate Klarsfeld, who was determined to confront the Nazi past of her parents' generation. She had already disrupted the German Bundestag by chanting: "Kiesinger, Nazi, Resign." In Germany, intergenerational tension was exacerbated by the lingering burden of National Socialism,[1] and the Adenauer era was an easy target. The student movement behind the social unrest of 1968 could no longer tolerate former Nazis holding government positions.

The scene that day marked a turning point. It would give pause to anyone who thought the past could still be silenced. Germans born in 1950, who later became the students of 1968, were the first generation of Germans who had not experienced the war, and they had no qualms about digging up that era. The old habit of placing blame on Hitler alone no longer satisfied them.

Beate Klarsfeld had looked forward to her confrontation with Kiesinger. She was a close friend of Günter Grass, who despised Kiesinger like he had despised Adenauer before him. The author of *The Tin Drum*, one of the most important works on the Third Reich, published in 1958, Grass was considered postwar Germany's "moral conscience." He won the Nobel

Prize in Literature in 1999. In 2006, however, on the eve of his eightieth birthday, Grass, who was promoting his memoirs, *Peeling the Onion*, was interviewed by *Frankfurter Allgemeine Zeitung* and he revealed that he had enlisted in the Waffen-SS in 1944 when he was seventeen. Grass told *Le Monde* in 2006: "It was tormenting me. My silence for so many years was one of the reasons why I wrote this book. I had to get it off my chest finally."[2]

In 1968, however, the year of Klarsfeld's slap in the face to the "Nazi father," Grass's Nazi past was still unknown. No one could have imagined that the intellectual guide of postwar Germany had himself been a Nazi soldier, and that he had hidden his membership in the Waffen-SS for half a century. Grass had tirelessly examined Nazi collaboration and guilt, as if echoing his own life. How could the same person who insisted on Germany's moral obligation to confront the past ever believe that time and his own fight could erase this indelible stain? His deliberate omission nearly cast a shadow over his entire life's work. One of Germany's most influential writers, Grass epitomizes both the country's silence and its difficulties breaking it and accepting the unacceptable.

The "Brandt years" would put an end to the idea that burying history was the only way to lay the foundations for German democracy. Chancellor Willy Brandt traveled to Poland on December 7, 1970, accompanied by Grass, who was one of his loyal supporters. There, on bended knee before the monument to the Warsaw Ghetto Uprising in 1943, he asked for forgiveness, in the name of the German people, for the Nazis' crimes, after which, he declared, famously: "I did what people do when words fail them." The historian Norbert Frei surmised it would take several generations for Germans to be able to look history and the extent of the Holocaust in the face because "knowing" something, Frei emphasized, is not the same as "dealing with it." In 1990, Frei argued that since the newest generations of Germans had no personal experience or memory of the war, and therefore were not guilty of its crimes, they should no longer be held morally and politically responsible.[3]

The closer to home something is, the harder it is to judge it objectively, as if recognizing the crimes of a father could irremediably sully the bonds of filial love. How difficult it must be for a child to admit, "My father was a monster and yet I loved him." Getting there is a long and fraught road.

Love that is stretched thin is more porous to judgment. This may be one reason why the least-loved children in this study, the ones who received little affection from their fathers, or spent very little time with them, judge their fathers the most severely. In the same way, the more distant the relation, in the case of nieces, nephews, and grandchildren, the easier it is to admit guilt. For Matthias Göring and Katrin Himmler, for example, the "monster" was a man they never knew.

Emotional intimacy is closely tied to temporal proximity. The passage of time and historical developments like the fall of the Berlin Wall have made it easier to face the past. The perception of Nazism, whether by the public or as developed by historians over the years, has evolved. As the truth came to light with time, children had no choice but to acknowledge Germany's history, and through that lens, their individual family stories, with all of the intergenerational silence those could hold.[4] The Nazi descendants whose lives are the focus of this book experienced Germany's silencing of the Nazi era. After the war, they became "the son or daughter of . . ." and they learned the undeniable facts of the Nazis' crimes, as seen through the eyes of the public. Their experiences at home, however, were much different. Their families could never deny their Nazi past, yet they hid the degree to which the fathers were involved in the Reich's murderous designs.

None of these children could ever say, "Papa wasn't a Nazi," to echo the title of the book by Harald Welzer, Sabine Möller, and Karoline Tschuggnall.[5] During the war, they were the children of war heroes; after the war, they were suddenly *Täter Kinder*, the children of criminals, although nothing had prepared them for this new world order in which they played the pariahs. Even as children, they could never have completely ignored that their fathers moved in circles of power that included Hitler himself. When they learned that Hitler was one of the greatest criminals history would ever know, they also understood they were intrinsically linked to him by a blood tie. Moreover, with the exception of Wolf Rüdiger Hess, Albert Speer Jr., and Rolf Mengele, they would never see their fathers again after Nuremberg, never be able to confront them, never ask them fundamental questions. Those who did have that opportunity often recoiled from the challenge. Yet every one of them had to face the fact that he or she was the child of a Nazi.

To move forward as adults, some chose to downplay their fathers' voluntary participation in the Nazis' war crimes. Others rejected outright their fathers and the love they felt for them. How a deep emotional bond can coexist with a profound sense of guilt is a complex and painful question. Whatever the nature of their relationship with their fathers, every one of them had to face society's reaction every time they made that relationship known.

For Germany to fully explore its past, the country would have to wait for the arrival of that first generation of Germans untouched by the war, as well as the leadership of Helmut Kohl as chancellor and the era of national reunification that began with the fall of the Berlin Wall on November 9, 1989. With East and West Germany reunified, the entire country could shoulder the guilt that had previously been contained to the principal actors of the Nazis' barbarism.

It is crucial, however, that a complete memory of Nazism is passed on to future generations. Horror can take many guises, as the rise of new forms of extremism proves. There will never be another Hitler but the events that hastened his appearance could very well be seen again. Can the past protect us from extremism, whatever its origins? It must be hoped. The generation of the Hitler Youth is dying out; four generations have followed it. It is no longer unthinkable to try to understand how any of us might have reacted in that era's social, economic, and legal context.

More than seventy years later, there are fewer and fewer remaining Nazi criminals and their victims, and soon there will be none left at all. When they are gone, the subjective memories of the participants of that era will also disappear. The names of the Reich's leaders must always serve as a warning for future generations, but all knowledge of the period must be preserved intact. Unfortunately, today's youth, whether out of disinterest or ignorance, is forgetting its history. Nevertheless, generalizations must be avoided; as Alexandra Oeser has shown, reactions to Nazism can vary widely depending on age, class, gender, political orientation, and education.[6]

The same holds true for these Nazi children. Whether they saw their fathers on a daily basis or only exchanged letters, they share a common history: they knew their fathers were National Socialists, but they only learned of their families' roles in the

Third Reich after the war from sources outside of their families. History left scant room to deny their fathers' actions, even though some did their utmost to believe it could be done. In all other respects, these children reacted in ways that are complex and unique to them individually as each came to terms with his or her family's history. Many factors contributed to these specific approaches, among them: gender, size of the family—whether the child had siblings or not—and intimacy with the parents—how affectionate or distant they were. Some of their stories share common characteristics, but each one is unique. The single common denominator is the impossibility of flouting one's family history: the price to pay is very high. Many of these children have made that task their life's work. Yet even Albert Speer Jr., whose professional achievements stand on their own, knows that the first question anyone ever asks him is in some way related to his father, Albert Speer.

Just as their fathers' destinies still haunt these children, the Nazi past lives on in our collective memory. Even when there are no more victims to bear witness and the Nazi hunts have receded into the past, their names will always be a reminder.

And so their stories have become history.

Notes

Introduction

1. Raimbault, Marie-Pierre and Michael Grynszpan, *Descendants de nazis: L'héritage infernal*, 2010, France: Bonne Pioche Télévision.
2. Bar-On, Dan, *L'Héritage du silence. Rencontres avec des enfants du III Reich*, preface by André Lévy, translated to French by F. Simon-Duneau, Paris, L'Harmattan, 2005, 191–193.
3. Gold, Tanya, "The Sins of Their Fathers," *The Guardian*, August 5, 2008, https://www.theguardian.com/world/2008/aug/06/judaism.secondworldwar.
4. Weber, Anne, *Vaterland*, Paris: Seuil, 2015.
5. Glass, Suzanne, "'Adolf Eichmann is a Historical Figure to Me.' Ricardo Eichmann speaks to Suzanne Glass about growing up the fatherless son of the Nazi war criminal hanged in Israel," *The Independent*, August 6, 1995.
6. Gilbert, G. M., *Nuremberg Diary*, New York: Farrar, Straus, 1947, 258.

7.   Arendt, Hannah, *Eichmann in Jerusalem*, New York: Viking, 1964, 16.

8.   Levi, Primo, "Primo Levi's Heartbreaking, Heroic Answers to the Most Common Questions He Was Asked About 'Survival in Auschwitz,'" *The New Republic*, February 17, 1986, https://newrepublic.com/article/119959/interview-primo-levi-survival-auschwitz.

9.   Arendt, *Eichmann in Jerusalem*, 134.

10. Ibid., 129.

11. Ibid., 134, 129.

12. Ibid., 16.

13. Ibid., 134.

14. Ibid., 17.

15. Ibid., 134.

16. Ibid., 26.

17. Ibid., 16.

18. Breitman, Richard, *The Architect of Genocide: Himmler and the Final Solution*, Hanover/London: Brandeis University Press, 1991, 243.

19. Welzer, Harald, *Les Exécuteurs: Des hommes normaux aux meurtriers de masse*, Paris: Gallimard, 2007, 42.

20. Gun, Nerin E., "Les enfants au nom maudit," *Historia* 241, December 1966, 55.

21. Speer, Albert, *Inside the Third Reich. Memoirs by Albert Speer*, trans. Richard and Clara Winston, New York: Macmillan, 1970, 92.

Gudrun Himler

1.   Kershaw, Ian, *Hitler, 1889–1936: Hubris,* New York: Norton, 2000, 568.

2.   A Waffen-SS division recruited from foreign volunteers.

3.   Gun, "Les enfants," 48.

4.   Ibid., 55.

5.   Himmler, Katrin and Michael Wildt, *Heinrich Himmler d'apres sa correspondence avec sa femme, 1927–1945*, Paris: Plon, 2014.

6.   Himmler and Wildt, *Heinrich Himmler d'apres sa correspondence avec sa femme,* 189

7.   Welzer, *Les Exécuteurs*, 184.

8. Lebert, Stephan and Norbert, *Car tu portes mon nom: Enfants de dirigeants Nazis, ils temoignent*, Paris: Plon, 2002, 38.

9. Longerich, Peter, *Heinrich Himmler*, trans. Jeremy Noakes and Lesley Sharpe, Oxford: Oxford University Press, 2012, 42–43.

10. Himmler and Wildt, *Heinrich Himmler d'apres sa correspondence avec sa femme*, 83.

11. Ibid., 13.

12. Journal of Margarete Himmler, dated January 30, 1940, USHMM, Acc.1999.A.0092.

13. Speer, *Inside the Third Reich*.

14. Kersten, Felix, *The Memoirs of Doctor Felix Kersten*, trans. Dr. Ernst Morwitz, New York: Doubleday, 1947.

15. Longerich, *Heinrich Himmler*, 376.

16. Fest, Joachim C., *The Face of the Third Reich: Portraits of the Nazi Leadership*, trans. Michael Bullock, New York: Da Capo Press, 1999, 271.

17. Sigmund, Anna Maria, *Les Femmes du III Reich*, Paris: Jean-Clause Lattès, 2004, 28.

18. Himmler's speech at Bad Tölz on February 18, 1937.

19. Moors, Markus and Moritz Pfeiffer, *Heinrich Himmlers Taschenkalender 1940*, Paderborn: Verlag Ferdinand Schöningh, 2013.

20. Journal of Margarete Himmler, dated May 3, 1939, USHMM, Acc.1999.A.0092.

21. Ibid.

22. Himmler, Katrin, *The Himmler Brothers: A German Family History*, trans. Michael Mitchell, London: Pan Books, 2008, 254.

23. Interrogation Records Prepared for War Crimes Proceedings at Nuremberg, 1945–1947, Content Source: NARA- Source Publication Year: 1984 - National Archives Catalog ID: 647749, National Archives Catalog Title: Reports, Interrogations, and Other Records Received from Various Allied Military Agencies, 1945–1948, Record Name: Himmler, Margarete.

24. Journal of Margarete Himmler, dated May 1, 1942, USHMM, Acc.1999.A.0092.

25. Ibid., March 7, 1940.

26. Interrogation Records Prepared for War Crimes Proceedings at Nuremberg, 1945–1947, Content Source: NARA, National Archives Catalog Title: Reports, Interrogations, and Other Records Received from Various Allied Military Agencies, 1945–1948, Publication Declassified: a: NND 760050 (1945–1949); NDD 760050 (1945–1949) | b: NARA | d: 1976 – Roll: 0006, Record Name: Himmler, Gudrun.

27. Ibid., May 18, 1940.

28. Ibid., September 6, 1943.

29. "Insight into the Orderly World of a Mass Murderer," *Die Welt*, January 25, 2014, https://www.welt.de/geschichte/himmler/article124223862/Insight-into-the-orderly-world-of-a-mass-murderer.html.

30. Ibid.

31. Himmler and Wildt, *Heinrich Himmler d'apres sa correspondence avec sa femme*, 279.

32. Ibid., 274.

33. Interrogation Records Prepared for War Crimes Proceedings at Nuremberg 1945–1947. Record Name: Margret Himmler.

34. Himmler and Wildt, *Heinrich Himmler d'apres sa correspondence avec sa femme*, 297–298.

35. Interrogation Records Prepared for War Crimes Proceedings at Nuremberg 1945–1947. Record Name: Gudrun Himmler.

36. Ibid.

37. Gun, "Les enfants," 48.

38. Ibid.

39. Interrogation Records Prepared for War Crimes Proceedings at Nuremberg 1945-1947. Record Name: Margret Himmler.

40. Gun, "Les enfants," 48.

41. Interrogation Records Prepared for War Crimes Proceedings at Nuremberg 1945–1947. Record Name: Gudrun Himmler, 5.

42. Stringer, Ann, "'No one loves a policeman,' Himmler's wife comments," *The Pittsburgh Press*, July 13, 1945.

43. Interrogation Records Prepared for War Crimes Proceedings at Nuremberg 1945–1947. Record Name: Margret Himmler, 14.

44. Interrogation Records Prepared for War Crimes Proceedings at Nuremberg 1945–1947. Record Name: Gudrun Himmler, 6.

45. Lebert and Lebert, *Car tu portes mon nom*, 144.

46. Gun, "Les enfants," 50.

47. Ibid.

48. Lebert, Stephan and Norbert, *Denn du trägst meinen Namen*, Karl Blessing Verlag, 2000. US edition: *My Father's Keeper* (op. cit.). French ed: *Car tu portes mon nom* (op. cit.).

49. Schröm, Oliver and Andrea Röpke, *Stille Hilfe für braune Kameraden: Das geheime Netzwerk der Alt-und Neonazis*, Berlin: Ch. Links Verlag, 2001, 47, 57, 191.

50. Sekkai, Kahina, "Gudrun Himmler, la 'Princesse du Nazisme,'" *Paris Match*, September 6, 2011.

51. Himmler, Katrin, *Die Brüder Himmler*, Fischer Taschenbuch Verlag, 2007. US edition: *The Himmler Brothers* (op. cit.).

52. Ibid.

53. Ibid, 306.

Edda Göring

1. Sigmund, *Les Femmes du III Reich*, 48.

2. Ibid., 45.

3. Lebert and Lebert, *Car tu portes mon nom*, 171.

4. Irving, David, *Göring: Le complice d'Hitler, 1933–1939*, Paris: Albin Michel, 1991.

5. Kershaw, *Hitler, 1889–1936*, 560.

6. Black, Conrad, *Franklin Delano Roosevelt: Champion of Freedom*, New York: Public Affairs, 2003, 697.

7. Speer, *Inside the Third Reich*, 259–260.

8. Ibid.

9. Fest, *The Face of the Third Reich*, 73.

10. Speer, *Inside the Third Reich*.

11. Göring, Emmy, *Göring: Le point de vue de sa femme*, Paris: Presses Pocket, 1965.

12. Irving, *Göring*, 230.

13. Feliciano, Hector, *The Lost Museum: The Nazi Conspiracy to Steal the*

World's Greatest Works of Art, trans. Tim Bent and the author, New York: Basic Books, 1995, 38.

14. Kersaudy, François, *Hermann Göring*, Paris: Perrin, 2010.
15. Kersaudy, François, "Goering doit être fusillé, mein Führer!" *Le Figaro Magazine*, July 26 2013.
16. Frischauer, Willi, *Goering*, London: Odhams Press, 1951, 265.
17. Göring, *Le point de vue de sa femme*, 180.
18. Ibid., 178–179.
19. Kersaudy, *Hermann Göring*.
20. Alexander Historical Auctions, Sale 47, Lot 49.
21. Manvell, Roger and Heinrich Fraenkel, *Goering: The Rise and Fall of the Notorious Nazi Leader*, London: Frontline, 2011, 396.
22. Bevan, Ian, "Frau Goering Secretly Held in Gaol," *Sydney Morning Herald*, November 20, 1945, 3.
23. Lebert and Lebert, *Car tu portes mon nom*, 203.
24. "Frau Goering Weeps: 'Bombing of Civilians is Terrible,'" *Argus*, July 14, 1945, 5.
25. Old Norse legends.
26. Kersaudy, *Hermann Göring*.
27. Ibid.
28. Göring, *Le point de vue de sa femme*, 229.
29. Sigmund, *Les Femmes du III Reich*, 98.
30. Kersaudy, *Hermann Göring*, 743.
31. Göring, *Le point de vue de sa femme*, 227.
32. Manvell and Fraenkel, *Goering*, 322
33. Göring, *Le point de vue de sa femme*, 230.
34. Frank, Niklas, *Meine deutsche Mutter*, Munich: Goldmann, 2006.
35. Letter from Emmy Göring, dated October 31, 1947, EMSO, 1048, Bayeriches Hauptstaadtsarchiv, Munich.
36. Göring, *Le point de vue de sa femme*, 245.
37. Auerbach, June 30, 1949, EMSO, 1048, Bayeriches Hauptstaadtsarchiv, Munich.
38. Kershaw, *Hitler*, 254–255
39. Gun, "Les enfants," 52.
40. Posner, Gerald, *Hitler's Children: Sons and Daughters of Leaders of*

the Third Reich Talk about Their Fathers and Themselves, New York: Random House, 1991.

41. Cojean, Annick, "Les mémoires du Shoah," *Le Monde*, April 29, 1995.

42. Morin, Roc, "An Interview with Nazi Leader Hermann Göring's Great-Niece: How do you cope with evil ancestry?" *The Atlantic*, October 16, 2013.

43. Elkins, Ruth, "Nazi Descendents: Mattias Göring Goes Kosher," *Der Spiegel Online International*, May 10, 2006.

Wolf R. Hess

1. Irving, David, *Hess: The Missing Years 1941–1945*, London: Focal Point, 2010, vi.

2. Speer, *Reich*, 175.

3. Irving, *Hess*, 4–5.

4. Hess, Ilse, *Rudolf Hess: Prisoner of Peace*, trans. Meyrick Booth, ed. George Pile, London: Britons, 1954.

5. Fest, *The Face of the Third Reich*, 193.

6. Ibid.

7. Kersten, *The Memoirs of Doctor Felix Kersten*, 65–66.

8. Irving, *Hess*, 37.

9. Ibid., 42.

10. Ibid., 37.

11. Ibid.

12. "Er spielte wieder mal den Toten: Gespräch mit Ilse Hess über Spandau-Häftling Rudolf Hess," *Der Spiegel*, November 20, 1967.

13. Gilbert, 12.

14. Kersaudy, François, *Les Secrets du IIIᵉ Reich*, Paris: Perrin, 2013, 160.

15. Ibid.

16. Interview with Wolf Rüdiger Hess: https://www.youtube.com/watch?v=ftWZgS75jDg.

17. Hess, Wolf Rüdiger, *My Father, Rudolf Hess*, trans. Frederick and Christine Crowley, London: W. H. Allen, 1986.

18. Hess, *Prisoner of Peace*, 48.

19. Gun, "Les enfants," 51.

20.   Irving, *Hess*, 330.

21.   Cooper, Abraham, "Rudolf Hess's Crime," *New York Times*, May 1, 1984.

22.   Hess, *Prisoner of Peace*, 83.

23.   Ibid., 143.

24.   Hess, *My Father*.

25.   Ibid.

26.   Hess, *My Father*.

27.   Medical Research Council Report, FO 1093/10.

28.   Kelley, Douglas M., *22 Männer um Hitler*, Olten/Bern: Delphi-Verlag, 1947.

29.   National Archives - M1270 - Interrogation records relating to the prosecution of war criminals in proceedings at Nuremberg, 1945–47. Record Name: Rudolf Hess.

30.   Ibid.

31.   Irving, *Hess*, 327.

32.   Hess, *My Father*; Hess, *Who Murdered My Father, Rudolf Hess? My Father's Mysterious Death in Spandau*, Editorial Revision, 1989; Hess, *Rudolf Hess: Ich bereue nichts*, (Graz: Stocker Leopold Verlag, 1994).

33.   Hess, *My Father*.

34.   Ibid.

35.   Ibid.

36.   Hess, *Prisoner of Peace*, 126–127.

37.   Manvell, Roger, Heinrich Fraenkel, *Hess: A Biography*, London: Granada, 1971, 189, 197.

38.   Hess, Wolf Rüdiger, "The Life and Death of My Father, Rudolf Hess," *Journal of Historical Review*, 13.1 (1993): 24–39.

39.   Schmemann, Serge, "Hess Is Buried Secretly by Family; Son Is Reported to Suffer Stroke," *New York Times*, August 25, 1987.

40.   Posner, *Hitler's Children*, 41.

41.   Cojean, "Les mémoires de la Shoah."

42.   Lebert and Lebert, 86–87.

43.   Mecklenburg, Jens, ed., *Handbuch deutscher Rechtsextremismus* , Berlin: Verlag GmbH, 1996, 299–302

44. "Nazi Leader's Grandson Fined Over Online Quotes," *Reuters*, January 24, 2002.

45. Lebert and Lebert, *Car tu portes mon nom*, 83.

Niklas Frank

1. Frank, Niklas, *Bruder Norman! "Mein Vater war ein Naziverbrecher, aber ich liebe ihn,"* Berlin: Dietz, 2013.

2. Frank, Niklas, interview with the author, September 8, 2015.

3. WWII Nuremberg Interrogation Records, Hans Frank, fold 3.

4. Frank, Niklas, *Der Vater: Eine Abrechung.* Munich: Goldman, 1993, 117.

5. Frank, Hans, *Im Angesicht des Galgens*, Munich-Grafelfing: Friedrich Alfred Beck, 1953.

6. Ibid.

7. Noakes, Jeremy and Geoffrey Pridham, *Nazism 1919–1945: Volume 2: State, Economy and Society 1933–1939*, Exeter: University of Exeter Press, 1983, 200.

8. Fest, *The Face of the Third Reich*, 210.

9. Picker, Henry, *Hitlers Tischgespräche im Führerhauptquartier*, Berlin: Propyläen Verlag, 2003, 225.

10. Kershaw, Ian, *The End: The Defiance and Destruction of Hitler's Germany, 1944–1945*, New York: Penguin, 2011, 214.

11. Schenk, Dieter, *Hans Frank: Hitlers Konjurist und Generalgouverneur*, Frankfurt: Fischer Verlag, 2006, 223.

12. Frank, Hans, *Im Angesicht des Galgens*.

13. Frank, interview with the author, September 8, 2015.

14. Ibid.

15. Frank, *Meine Deutsche Mutter*.

16. Malaparte, Curzio, *Kaputt*, Paris: Gallimard, October 26, 1972, Folio, 99.

17. Frank, *Bruder Norman*, 64.

18. Frank, interview with the author, September 8, 2015.

19. Ibid.

20. Ibid.

21. Malaparte, *Kaputt*, 99.

22. Frank, interview with the author, September 8, 2015.
23. Ibid.
24. Frank, *Der Vater*.
25. Frank, *Bruder Norman*.
26. Longerich, *Heinrich Himmler*, 564.
27. Kershaw, *The End*, 214.
28. Frank, *Bruder Norman*.
29. Frank, interview with the author, September 8, 2015.
30. Lebert and Lebert, *Car tu portes mon nom*, 127.
31. Housden, Martin, *Hans Frank: Lebensraum and the Holocaust*, New York: Palgrave Macmillan, 2003, 151.
32. Frank, interview with the author, September 8, 2015.
33. Gilbert, *Nuremberg Diary*, 21.
34. Frank, interview with the author, September 8, 2015.
35. Posner, *Hitler's Children*, 33.
36. Ibid., 33–34.
37. Ibid., 34.
38. Ibid., 34–35.
39. Cojean, "Les mémoires de la Shoah."
40. Frank, interview with the author, September 8, 2015.
41. Gilbert, *Nuremberg Diary*, 116.
42. Frank, interview with the author, September 8, 2015.
43. Posner, *Hitler's Children*, 34.
44. Lewis, Jon E., *The Mammoth Book of Eyewitness World War II*, New York: Carroll & Graf, November 11, 2002, 565.
45. Frank, interview with the author, September 8, 2015.
46. Frank, *Meine Deutsche Mutter*, 416.
47. Ibid.
48. Ibid., 441
49. Ibid.
50. Ibid., 451.
51. Frank, interview with the author, September 8, 2015.
52. Ibid.
53. Ibid.
54. Ibid.

55. Ibid.

56. Ibid.

57. Schwabe, Alexandre, "Interview mit Niklas Frank zur Speer-Debatte: 'Das ewige Herumgeschmuse der Kinder ist lächerlich,'" *Der Spiegel* Online, May 13, 2005.

58. Schwabe, "Interview mit Niklas Frank zur Speer-Debatte."

59. Frank, interview with the author, September 8, 2015.

60. Ibid.

61. Ibid.

62. Frank, *Der Vater*, 12.

63. Schwabe, "Interview mit Niklas Frank zur Speer-Debatte."

64. Frank, interview with the author, September 8, 2015.

65. Frank, *Meine deutsche Mutter.*

66. Cojean, "Les mémoires de la Shoah."

67. Frank, interview with the author, September 8, 2015.

68. Frank, *Meine deutsche Mutter.*

69. Frank, interview with the author, September 8, 2015.

70. Frank, *Bruder Norman.*

71. Frank, interview with the author, September 8, 2015.

72. Frank, *Bruder Norman*, 69.

73. Ibid.

74. Posner, *Hitler's Children*, 21.

75. Frank, *Bruder Norman*, 83.

76. Posner, *Hitler's Children*, 39.

77. Michaeslen, Sven, "Niklas Frank," *Süddeutsche Zeitung*, no. 11, 2014.

78. Ze'evi, Chanoch, *Hitler's Children* (Israel: Film Movement, 2012), DVD.

79. Frank, interview with the author, September 8, 2015.

80. Schwabe, "Interview mit Niklas Frank zur Speer-Debatte."

Martin Adolf Bormann Jr.

1. Fest, *The Face of the Third Reich*, 127.

2. Bormann, Martin, *Leben gegen Schatten*, Patterborn: Bonifatius, 2000.

3. Sigmund, *Les Femmes du III Reich*, 19.

4. Speer, *Inside the Third Reich*, 146.

5. Fest, *The Face of the Third Reich*, 271.

6. Kershaw, *The End*, 242.

7. Rosenberg's *The Myth of the Twentieth Century* was considered a foundational text of National Socialism and was the second most read book in the Third Reich after *Mein Kampf.*

8. Bormann, *Leben gegen Schatten.*

9. Ibid., 70–71.

10. Ibid., 49.

11. Bar-On, *L'Héritage du silence*, 188.

12. Ibid., 181.

13. Ibid., 190–191.

14. Bormann, *Leben gegen Schatten*, 83.

15. Speer, *Inside the Third Reich*, 96.

16. Bar-On, *L'Héritage du silence*, 192.

17. In 2011, the Austrian press published revelations that while he was a teacher at the school of the Missionaries of the Sacred Heart in Salzburg in the 1960s, Martin Adolf had repeatedly raped, sexually assaulted, and physically harmed a certain Victor M. Other students who were questioned in the case alleged that he had beaten them until they were bloody and, for one student, until he was unconscious. Martin Adolf vigorously denied these accusations.

18. Lebert and Lebert, *Car tu portes mon nom*, 97

19. Bormann, *Leben gegen Schatten*, 196.

20. Lebert and Lebert, *Car tu portes mon nom;* 96–97

21. Bormann, *Leben gegen Schatten*, 196.

22. Ibid., 261.

The Höss Children

1. Interrogation of Rudolf Höss at Nuremberg, April 15, 1946.

2. Höss, Rudolf, Pery Broad, and Johann Paul Kremer, *Auschwitz as Seen by the SS*, eds. Jadwiga Bezwinska, Danuta Czech, trans. Constantine Fitzgibbon, Krystyna Michalik, New York: H. Fertig, 1984, 19.

3. Prisoners in the concentration camps wore colored triangles to

indicate the reason for their detention: red for political prisoners; green for common criminals; black for people considered "asocial," such as the mentally ill; purple for Jehovah's Witnesses; and pink for homosexuals.

4. Harding, Thomas, *Hanns and Rudolf: The True Story of the German Jew Who Tracked Down and Caught the Commandant of Auschwitz*, New York: Simon & Schuster, 2013, 103.

5. Höss et al., *Auschwitz as Seen by the SS*, 19.

6. Arendt, Hannah, *Antisemitism: Part One of the Origins of Totalitarianism*, New York: Schocken Books, 1951.

7. Gilbert, *Nuremberg Diary*, 258.

8. Höss, Rudolf, *Kommandant in Auschwitz: Autobiographische Aufzeichnungendes*, Munich: Martin Broszat, 1963; *Death Dealer: The Memoirs of the SS Kommandant at Auschwitz*, ed. Steven Paskuly, trans. Andrew Pollinger , Buffalo: Prometheus Books, 1992, 186.

9. Ibid., 50.

10. Gilbert, *Nuremberg Diary*, 251.

11. Ibid., 258.

12. Höss, *Death Dealer*, 83.

13. Gilbert, *Nuremberg Diary*, 260.

14. Höss, *Death Dealer*, 122.

15. Ibid., 125.

16. Höss may have incorrectly remembered the date of Himmler's orders for the Final Solution.

17. Gilbert, *Nuremberg Diary*, 250.

18. Ibid., 250.

19. Hilberg, Raul, *The Destruction of the European Jews, Volume One*, New York: Holmes & Meier Publishers, 1985, 192.

20. Höss, *Death Dealer*, 28.

21. Ibid.

22. Ibid., 161.

23. Fest, *The Face of the Third Reich*, 283–284.

24. Höss et al., *Auschwitz as Seen by the SS*, 156.

25. Cronin, Frances, "Nazi Legacy: The Troubled Descendants," *BBC Magazine*, May 23, 2012.

26. Gilbert, *Nuremberg Diary*, 259.

27. Höss et al., *Auschwitz as Seen by the SS*, 292.

28. Ibid., 291.

29. Ibid., 294.

30. "Report of Janina Szczurek," in Höss et al., *Auschwitz as Seen by the SS*, 294.

31. Höss, *Death Dealer*, 156.

32. Höss et al., *Auschwitz as Seen by the SS*, 43.

33. Höss, *Death Dealer*,163.

34. Ibid., 164.

35. Höss et al., *Auschwitz as Seen by the SS*, 288.

36. Ibid., 194

37. Gilbert, *Nuremberg Diary*, 259.

38. Höss, *Kommandant in Auschwitz*, 221.

39. Höss, *Death Dealer*, 186.

40. Ibid., 185.

41. Harding, *Hanns et Rudolf*, 271–272.

42. Ibid., 275.

43. Harding, Thomas, "Hiding in N. Virginia, a Daughter of Auschwitz," *Washington Post*, September 7, 2013.

44. Anderson, Graham, "My Nazi Family," *Exberliner*, May 6, 2014.

45. Lianos, Konstaninos, "Auschwitz's Commander's Grandson: Why My Family Call Me a Traitor," *The Telegraph*, November 20, 2014.

46. Lianos, "Auschwitz's Commander's Grandson."

47. Eldad, Beck, "Ghouls cash in on Auschwitz as death camp crumbles away," *Express*, May 18, 2011, http://www.express.co.uk/expressyourself/201830/Ghouls-cash-in-on-Auschwitz-as-death-camp-crumbles-away.

48. Harding, "Hiding in N. Virginia."

The Speer Children

1. Smoltczyk, Alexander, "2022 World Cup in Qatar: The Desert Dreams of German Architect Albert Speer," *Der Spiegel*, June 1, 2012.

2. Speer, Albert, Jr., *Die intelligente Stadt*, Stuttgart: Deutsche Verlags-Anstalt, 1992.

3. Beyer, Susanne, "Improving on the Nazi Past: Albert Speer's Son, Urban Planner," *Der Spiegel*, December 21, 2007.

4. Smoltczyk, "2022 World Cup in Qatar."

5. Beyer, "Improving on the Nazi Past."

6. Khrushsheva, Nina, "Olympic Hubris: Albert Speer's Son Helped Design the Architecture of the Beijing Games, but the Similarities with Berlin 1936 Don't End There," *The Guardian*, August 7, 2008.

7. Millot, Lorraine, "Albert Speer, 63 ans, est architecte. Comme son homonyme de père, le bâtisseur de Hitler. Mais lui a choisi le Francfort la libérale. Tel père, quel fils?" *Libération*, February 10, 1998.

8. Interview with Albert Speer Jr., https://www.youtube.com/watch?v=033OGnfRKJY.

9. Matzig, Gerhard, "Hitler war für uns ein netter Onkel," *Süddeutsche Zeitung*, May 20, 2010.

10. Speer, *Inside the Third Reich*, 112.

11. Trevor-Roper, Hugh, *The Last Days of Hitler*, Chicago: University of Chicago Press, 1992, 269.

12. Speer, *Inside the Third Reich*, 14.

13. Ibid.

14. Ibid., 18–19.

15. Ibid., 18.

16. Schaal, Hans Dieter, *Hans Dieter Schaal, In-between: Exhibition Architecture*, Stuttgart: Edition Axel Menges, 1999, 14.

17. Speer, Albert, *Journal de Spandau*, Paris: Robert Laffont, 1976, 156.

18. Matzig, "Hitler war für uns ein netter Onkel."

19. Speer, *Inside the Third Reich*, 17.

20. Nissen, Margret, *Sind Sie die Tochter Speer?*, Cologne: Bastei Lübbe, 2005; München: Deutsche Verlags-Anstalt, 2005.

21. Speer, *Journal de Spandau*, 76.

22. Schramm, Hilde, *Meine Lehrerin, Dr. Dora Lux 1882–1959*, Reinbek: Rowohlt Verlag, 2012.

23. Interview with Arnold Speer, https://www.youtube.com/watch?v=033OGnfRKJY.

24. Speer, *Inside the Third Reich*, 516.

25.   Sereny, Gitta, *Albert Speer. His Battle with Truth*, New York: Vintage, 1996.

26.   Fest, Joachim C., *Speer: The Final Verdict*, trans. Ewald Osers, Alexandra Dring, New York: Harcourt, 2002, 281.

27.   Fest, *Speer: The Final Verdict*, 311

28.   Speer, *Journal de Spandau*, 218.

29.   Fest, *Speer*, 314.

30.   Sereny, *Albert Speer*, 336.

31.   Fest, *Speer*, 314.

32.   Nissen, *Sind Sie die Tochter Speer?*.

33.   Speer, *Journal de Spandau*, 163.

34.   Bundesarchiv Koblenz, Article B122/28025.

35.   Sereny, *Albert Speer*, 651–652.

36.   Hamrén, Henrik, "I Feel Ashamed," *The Guardian*, April 17, 2005.

37.   Gilbert, *Nuremberg Diary*, 24–25.

38.   Van der Vat, Dan, *The Good Nazi: The Life and Lies of Albert Speer*, New York: Houghton Mifflin, 1997, 6.

39.   Ibid.

40.   Speer, *Journal de Spandau*, 321.

41.   Fest, *Speer*, 315.

42.   Sereny, *Albert Speer*, 643.

43.   Speer, *Journal de Spandau*, 548

44.   Nissen, *Sind Sie die Tochter Speer?*, 59

45.   Ibid., 159

46.   Millot, "Albert Speer, 63 ans, est architecte."

47.   Norden, Eric, "Albert Speer, Hitler's Architect," *Playboy* 18 no. 6, June 1971, 69.

48.   Ibid.

49.   Sereny, *Albert Speer*, 706.

50.   Speer, *Journal de Spandau*, 93.

51.   Raben, Mia, "MS - Vergangenheit: Der lebenslange Schatten," *Der Spiegel*, February 7, 2004.

52.   Hamrén, "I Feel Ashamed."

53.   Ibid.

54.   Ibid.

55. Speer, *Journal de Spandau*, 219.
56. Hamrén, "I Feel Ashamed."
57. Nissen, *Sind Sie die Tochter Speer?*, 159.
58. Speer, *Inside the Third Reich*, 112.

Rolf Mengele

1. Alexander Historical Auctions, Sale 45, July 21, 2011, Lot 4: "The Hidden Journals of Dr. Josef Mengele," Full Detail, http://auctions. alexautographs.com/auction-lot-detail/THE-HIDDEN-JOURNALS-OF-DR.-JOSEF-MENGELE---Hammer-Price:-$24&salelot=45++++++++++4+&refno=+++70337.
2. Ibid., Lot 650 dated July 31, 1960–April 26, 1962.
3. Aderet, Ofer, "In His Diary Mengele Predicted 90% of Humans Would Die of Stupidity," *Haaretz*, February 2, 2010, http://www. haaretz.com/in-his-diary-mengele-predicted-90-of-humans-would-die-of-stupidity-1.262577.
4. Posner, Gerald L. and John Ware, *Mengele: The Complete Story*, New York: Cooper Square Press, 2000, 234–235.
5. Mengele, Rolf, interview with Gerald Posner, 1985.
6. Hilberg, Raul, *The Destruction of the European Jews, Volume III*, New Haven: Yale University Press, 2003, 1011.
7. Posner and Ware, *Mengele*, 25.
8. Ibid.
9. Ibid.
10. Sereny, *Albert Speer*, 467.
11. Mengele interview with Gerald Posner, 1985.
12. "In the Matter of Josef Mengele. A Report to the Attorney General of the United States," October 1992.
13. Posner and Ware, *Mengele*, xvii.
14. Rolf Mengele, interview with Gerald Posner, 1985.
15. Ibid.
16. Posner, *Hitler's Children*, 128.
17. Ibid., 130.
18. Henry, Marc, "Comment le Mossad a rate la capture de Josef Mengele," *Le Figaro*, Sept 4, 2008.

19.   "In the Matter of Josef Mengele. A Report to the Attorney General of the United States," October 1992.

20.   Jessen, Norbert, "Vati, der Massenmörder. Die israelische Zeitung 'Jedioth' veröffentlicht ein Interview mit Rolf Mengele," *Die Welt*, May 8, 2008.

Conclusion

1.   Jessen, Norbert, "Vati, der Massenmörder."

2.   "Le prix Nobel de littérature Günter Grass a servi dans les Waffen-SS," *Le Monde*, August 12, 2006, http://www.lemonde.fr/culture/article/2006/08/12/le-prix-nobel-de-litterature-gunter-grass-a-servi-dans-les-waffen-ss_803111_3246.html.

3.   Frei, Norbert, "L'Holocaust dans l'historiographie allemande, un point aveugle dans la conscience historique," *Vingtième Siècle: Revue d'histoire*, 34 (1992): 157–162.

4.   Welzer, Harald, Sabine Möller, and Karoline Tschuggnall, *Opa war kein Nazi. Nationalsozialismus und Holocaust im Familiengedächtnis*, Frankfurt: Fischer Taschenbuch Verlag, 2002.

5.   Ibid.

6.   Oeser, Alexandra, *Enseigner Hitler: Les adolescents allemands face au passé nazi en Allemagne. Appropriations, interprétations et usages de l'histoire*, Paris: Editions de la Maison des sciences de l'homme, 2010.

Sources from Archives

Gudrun Himmler

Dossier of Margarete Himmler, Bundesarchiv Berlin : 413877

Interrogation Records Prepared for War Crimes Proceedings at Nuremberg, 1945–1947, Content Source: NARA: National Archives Catalog Title: Reports, Interrogations, and Other Records Received from Various Allied Military Agencies, 1945–1948, Publication Declassified: a: NND 760050 (1945–1949); NDD 760050 (1945–1949) | b: NARA | d: 1976 – Roll: 0006, Record Name: Himmler, Gudrun.

Interrogation Records Prepared for War Crimes Proceedings at Nuremberg, 1945–1947 – Content Source: NARA, Source Publication Year: 1984, National Archives Catalog ID: 647749, National Archives Catalog Title: Reports, Interrogations, and Other Records Received from Various Allied Military Agencies, 1945–1948, Record Name: Himmler, Margarete.

Journal of Margarete Himmler – USHMM, Acc.1999.A.0092.

Edda Göring
A letter from Emmy Göring, Munich, Bayeriches Hauptstaadtsarchiv, October 31 1947. Auerbach, June 1949, EMSO, 1048, Bayeriches Hauptstaadtsarchiv, Munich. Dossier of Emmy Göring, nee Sonnemann, Bundesarchiv Berlin: 109673.

Wolf R. Hess
Dossier of Ilse Hess, Bundesarchiv Berlin : 381330
Interrogation Records Prepared for War Crimes Proceedings at Nuremberg, 1945–1947, Content Source: NARA, Source Publication Year: 1984, National Archives Catalog Title: Reports, Interrogations, and Other Records Received from Various Allied Military Agencies, 1945–1948, Publication Declassified : a : NDD 760050 (1945–1949) ; NDD 760050 (1945–1949) | b: NARA | d: 1976 – Roll: 0006, Record Name: Hess, Rudolf.

Martin Adolf Bormann
Institute of Contemporary History, Munich. ZS 1701/1 Bestand Bormann Adolf Martin.

Rudolf Höss
Interrogation of Rudolf Höss – April 15 1946 – Nuremberg Trial Proceedings vol. 11, http://avalon.law.yale.edu/imt/04-14-46.asp.
Interrogation Records Prepared for War Crimes Proceedings at Nuremberg, 1945–1947,Content Source: NARA, Source Publication Year: 1984, Fold 3 Publication Year: 2009, National Archives Catalog ID: 647749, National Archives Catalog Title: Reports, Interrogations, and Other

Records Received from Various Allied Military Agencies, 1945–1948, Publication Declassified: a : NDD 760050 (1945–1949); NDD 760050 (1945–1949) | b: NARA | d: 1976, Record Name: Höss, Rudolf.

Other Sources

"In the matter of Josef Mengele: A report to the Attorney General of the United States," US Department of Justice, Office of Special Investigations, October 1992.

Bundesarchive Koblenz – Article B122/28025.

BIBLIOGRAPHY

Aderet, Ofer, "In His Diary Mengele Predicted 90% of Humans Would Die of Stupidity," *Haaretz*, February 2, 2010, http://www.haaretz.com/in-his-diary-mengele-predicted-90-of-humans-would-die-of-stupidity-1.262577.

Akyol, Cigdem, "Ein volk, das nichts kapiert hat," *Weiner Zeitung*, July 7, 2013.

Anderson, Graham, "My Nazi Family," *Exberliner*, May 6, 2014.

Arendt, Hannah, *Eichmann in Jerusalem: A Report on the Banality of Evil*, New York: Viking, 1964. Print.

—, *Antisemitism: Part One of the Origins of Totalitarianism*, New York: Schocken Books, 1951.

Bar-On, Dan, *L'Héritage du silence: Rencontres avec des enfants du III Reich*, preface by André Lévy, translated to French by F. Simon-Duneau, Paris: L'Harmattan, 2005; *Legacy of*

Silence: Encounters with Children of the Third Reich, Cambridge: Harvard University Press, 1989.

Beven, Ian, "Frau Goering Secretly Held in Gaol," *The Sydney Morning Herald*, November 20, 1945, 3.

—, "Goering Faces Judges as 'Man of Peace,'" *The Sydney Morning Herald*, November 20 1945, 1.

Beyer, Susanne, "Der unischtbare Riese," *Der Spiegel*, December 17, 2007.

—, "Improving on the Nazi Past: Albert Speer's Son, Urban Planner," *Der Spiegel*, December 21, 2007.

Black, Conrad, *Franklin Delano Roosevelt: Champion of Freedom*, New York: Public Affairs, 2003.

Bormann, Martin, *Hitler's Table Talk Third Edition*, Create Space Independent Publishing Platform, 2013.

—, *Leben gegen Schatten*, Paderborn: Bonifatius, 2003.

Breitman, Richard, *The Architect of Genocide: Himmler and the Final Solution*, Hanover/London: Brandeis University Press, 1991.

Brinks, Jan Herman, Edward Timms, and Stella Rock, *Nationalist Myths and the Modern Media: Contested Identities in the Age of Globalization*, New York: I. B. Tauris, 2005.

Browning, Christopher R., *Ordinary Men: Reserve Police Battalion 101 and the Final Solution in Poland*, New York: HarperCollins, 1992.

Cojean, Annick, "Les mémoires de la Shoah," *Le Monde*, April 29, 1995.

Cooper, Abraham, "Rudolf Hess's Crime," *New York Times*, May 1, 1984.

Cronin, Frances, "Nazi Legacy: The Troubled Descendants," *BBC Magazine*, May 23, 2012.

Dörfler, Thomas and Klärner Andreas, "Rudolf Hess as Martyr

for Germany: The Reinterpretation of Historical Figures in National Discourse," *Nationalist Myths and Modern Media: Cultural Idenity in the Age of Globalization*, Jan Herman Brinks, Edward Timms, and Stella Rock, eds, New York/London: I. B. Tauris, 2005, 139–152.

Eldad, Beck, "Ghouls Cash in on Auschwitz as Death Camp Crumbles Away," *Express*, May 18, 2011, http://www.express.co.uk/expressyourself/201830/Ghouls-cash-in-on-Auschwitz-as-death-camp-crumbles-away.

Elkins, Ruth, "Nazi Descendents: Matthias Göring Goes Kosher," *Der Spiegel Online International*, May 10, 2006, http://www.spiegel.de/international/nazi-descendents-matthias-goering-goes-kosher-a-415430.html.

"Er spielte wieder mal den Toten: Gespräch mit Ilse Hess über Spandau-Häftling Rudolf Hess," *Der Spiegel*, November 20, 1967, http://www.spiegel.de/spiegel/print/d-46196217.html.

Feliciano, Hector, *Le Musee disparu: Enquete sur le pillage d'oeuvres d'art en France par les Nazis*, Paris: Gallimard, 2012; *The Lost Museum: The Nazi Conspiracy to Steal the World's Greatest Works of Art*, trans. Tim Bent and the author, New York: Basic Books, 1995.

Fest, Joachim C., *The Face of the Third Reich: Portraits of the Nazi Leadership*, trans. Michael Bullock, New York: Da Capo Press, 1999.

—, *Speer: The Final Verdict*, trans. Ewald Osers, Alexandra Dring, New York: Harcourt, 2002.

Frank, Hans, *Im Angesicht des Galgens*, Munich-Grafelfing: Friedrich Alfred Beck, 1953.

—, *Das Diensttagebuch des deutschen Generalgouverneurs in Polen, 1939–1945*, eds. Werner Prag and Wolfgang Jacobmayer, Stuttgart: Deutsche Verlags-Anstalt, 1975.

Frank, Niklas, *Bruder Norman! "Mein Vater war ein Naziverbre-cher, aber ich liebe ihn,"* Berlin: Dietz, 2013.

—, *Der Vater: Eine Abrechnung*, Munich: Goldmann, 1993;

—, interview with the author, September 8, 2015.

—, *Meine deutsche Mutter*, Munich: Goldman, 2006.

"Frau Goering Weeps: 'Bombing of Civilians is Terrible,'" *Argus*, July 14, 1945.

Frei, Norbert, "L'Holocauste dans l'historiographie allemande, un point avegule dans la conscience historique?" *Vingtiéme Siècle: Reue d'histoire* 34, 1992.

Freidländer, Saul, *L'Allemagne nazie et les Juifs: Les Années d'extermination*, trans. P. E. Dauzat, Paris: Seiul, 2008; *The Years of Extermination: Nazi Germany and the Jews, 1939–1945*, New York: Harper, 2007.

Frischauer, Willi, *Goering*, London: Odhams Press, 1951.

Gilbert, G. M., *Nuremberg Diary*, New York: Farrar, Straus, 1947.

Glass, Suzanne, "'Adolf Eichmann is a Historical Figure to Me.' Ricardo Eichmann speaks to Suzanne Glass about growing up the fatherless son of the Nazi war criminal hanged in Israel," *The Independent*, August 6, 1995.

Gold, Tanya, "The Sins of Their Fathers," *The Guardian*, August 6, 2008.

Göring, Emmy, *Göring: Le point de vue de sa femme*, Paris: Presses Pocket, 1965.

Gun, Nerin E., "Les enfants au nom maudit," *Historia* 241, December 1966.

Haarer, Johanna, *Die deutsche Mutter und ihr letztes Kind: die Autobiographien der erfolgreichsten NS-Erzeihungsexpertin und ihrer jüngsten Tochter*, Hanover: Offizin Verlag, 2012.

Hamrén, Henrik, "I Feel Ashamed," *The Guardian*, April 17, 2005.

Harding, Thomas, *Hanns et Rudolf: Comment un Juif allemande min fin à la cavale du commandant d'Auschwitz*, Paris: Flammarion, 2014; *Hanns and Rudolf: The True Story of the German Jew Who Tracked Down and Caught the Commandant of Auschwitz*, New York: Simon & Schuster, 2013.

—, "Hiding in N. Virginia, a Daughter of Auschwitz," *Washington Post*, September 7, 2013.

Hanisch, Ernst, *L'Obersalzberg*, ed. by the Berchtesgadener Land Foundation.

Hanitzsch, Konstanze, *Deutsche Scham: Gender, Medien, "Taterkinder," ein Analyse der Auseinandersetzungen von Niklas Frank, Beate Niemann, und Malte Ludin*, Berlin: Metropol, 2013.

Heidemann, Gerd, "Die Millionen hat Kujau," *Vanity Fair*, November 2008.

—, *Rudolf Hess: Prisoner of Peace*, trans. Meyrick Booth, ed. George Pile, London: Britons, 1954.

Henry, Marc, "Comment le Mossad a rate la capture de Josef Mengele," *Le Figaro*, Sept 4, 2008.

Hess, Wolf Rüdiger, *My Father, Rudolf Hess*, trans. Frederick and Christine Crowley, London: W. H. Allen & Co., 1986.

—, *Who Murdered My Father, Rudolf Hess? My Father's Mysterious Death in Spandau*, Buenos Aires: Editorial Revision, 1989.

—, *Rudolf Hess: Ich bereue nichts*, Graz: Stocker Leopold Verlag, 1994.

—, "The Life and Death of My Father, Rudolf Hess," *The Journal of Historical Review* 13:1, 1993, 24–29.

Hilberg, Raul, *The Destruction of the European Jews, Volume I*, New York: Holmes & Meier Publishers, 1985.

—, *The Destruction of the European Jews, Volume III*, New Haven: Yale University Press, 2003.

Himmler, Katrin, *Die Brüder Himmler*, Berlin: Fischer Taschenbuch Verlag, 2007; *The Himmler Brothers: A German Family History*, trans. Michael Mitchell, London: Pan Books, 2008.

Himmler, Katrin and Michael Wildt, *Heinrich Himmler d'apres sa correspondence avec sa femme, 1927–1945*, Paris: Plon, 2014; *The Private Heinrich Himmler: Letters of a Mass Murderer*, trans. Thomas S. and Abby J. Hansen, New York: St. Martin's Press, 2016.

—, *Himmler privat: Briefe eines Massenmörders*, Munich: Piper Verlag, 2014.

Höss, Rudolf, *Kommandant in Auschwitz. Autobiographische Aufzeichnungendes*, Munich: Martin Broszat, 1963; *Death Dealer: The Memoirs of the SS Kommandant at Auschwitz*, ed. Steven Paskuly, trans. Andrew Pollinger, Buffalo: Prometheus Books, 1992.

Höss, Rudolf, Pery Broad, and Johann Paul Kremer, *Auschwitz vu par les SS*, Oświęcim: Edition du Musée d'Etat, 1974; *Auschwitz as Seen by the SS*, eds. Jadwiga Bezwinska, Danuta Czech, trans. Constantine Fitzgibbon, Krystyna Michalik, New York: Howard Fertig Publisher, 1984.

Housden, Martin, *Hans Frank: Lebensraum and the Holocaust*, New York: Palgrave Macmillan, 2003.

Husson, Edouard, *Heydrich et la Solution finale*, preface by Ian Kershaw, Paris: Perrin, 2012.

"Insight into the Orderly World of a Mass Murderer," *Die*

Welt, January 25, 2014, https://www.welt.de/geschichte/himmler/article124223862/Insight-into-the-orderly-world-of-a-mass-murderer.html.

Interview with Wolf Rüdiger Hess, YouTube, May 11, 2011, https://www.youtube.com/watch?v=ftWZgS75jDg.

Irving, David, *Göring: Le complice d'Hitler, 1933–1939*, Paris: Albin Michel, 1991; *Göring: A Biography*, New York: William Morrow & Co, 1989.

—, *Hess: The Missing Years 1941–1945*, London: Focal Point, 2010.

Jessen, Norbert, "Vati, der Massenmörder. Die israelische Zeitung 'Jedioth' veröffentlicht ein Interview mit Rolf Mengele," *Die Welt*, May 8, 2008.

Jürgen, Matthäus, "'Es war sehr nett.' Auszüge aus dem Tagebuch der Margarete Himmler, 1937–1935," *Werkstatt Geschichte*, 2000, 1992.

Kellenbach, Batharina von, *The Mark of Cain: Guilt and Denial in the Post-War Lives of Nazi Perpetrators*, Oxford University Press USA, July 25 2013, 304.

Kelley, Douglas M., *22 Männer um Hitler*, Olten/Bern: Delphi-Verlag, 1947.

Kersaudy, François, *Hermann Göring*, Paris: Perrin, 2010.

—, "Goering doit être fusillé, mein Führer!" *Le Figaro*, July 26, 2013.

—, *Les Secrets du IIIᵉ Reich*, Paris: Perrin, 2013.

Kershaw, Ian, *Fateful Choices: Ten Decisions that Changed the World, 1940–1941*, London: Penguin Books, 2007.

—, *Hitler, 1889–1936: Hubris*, New York: Norton, 2000.

—, *Le Mythe Hitler*, Paris: Flammarion, 2006.

—, *Popular Opinion and Political Dissent in the Third Reich: Bavaria, 1933–1975*, Oxford: Oxford University Press, 1983.

—, *The End: The Defiance and Destruction of Hitler's Germany, 1944–1945*, New York: Penguin, 2011.

Kersten, Felix, *The Memoirs of Doctor Felix Kersten*, trans. Dr. Ernst Morwitz, New York: Doubleday, 1947.

Khrushsheva, Nina, "Olympic Hubris: Albert Speer's Son Helped Design the Architecture of the Beijing Games, but the similarities with Berlin 1936 Don't End There," *The Guardian*, August 7, 2008.

Klabunde, Anja, *Magda Goebbels: Approche d'une vie*, trans. S. Bénistan, Paris: Tallandier, 2011.

"Le prix Nobel de littérature Günter Grass a servi dans les Waffen-SS," *Le Monde*, August 12, 2006.

Lebert, Stephan and Norbert, *Car tu portes mon nom. Enfants de dirigeants Nazis, ils temoignent*, Paris: Plon, 2002; *Denn du trägst meinen Namen*, Munich: Karl Blessing Verlag, 2000. *My Father's Keeper: Children of Nazi Leaders: An Intimate History of Damage and Denial*, trans. Julien Evans, Boston: Little, Brown, 2001.

Leeb, Johannes, *Wir waren Hitlers Elitschüler: ehemalige Zöglinge der NS-Ausleseschulen brechen irh Schweigen*, Hambourg: Rasch und Röhring, 1998.

Levi, Primo, "Primo Levi's Heartbreaking, Heroic Answers to the Most Common Questions He Was Asked About 'Survival in Auschwitz,'" *The New Republic*, February 17, 1986.

—, *Si c'est un homme*, French trans. M. Schruoffeneger, Paris: Julliard, 1987.

Lewis, Jon E., *The Mammoth Book of Eyewitness World War II*, New York: Carroll & Graf, November 11, 2002.

Lianos, Konstaninos, "Auschwitz's Commander's Grandson:

Why My family Call Me a Traitor," *The Telegraph*, November 20, 2014.

Longerich, Peter, *Heinrich Himmler*, trans. Jeremy Noakes and Lesley Sharpe, Oxford: Oxford University Press, 2012.

—, *Nous ne savions pas: Les Allemands et la Solution finale*, French trans. R. Clarinard, Paris: Héloïse d'Ormesson, 2010.

Malaparte, Curzio, *Kaputt*, Paris: Gallimard, October 26, 1972.

Manvell, Roger and Heinrich Fraenkel, *Goering: The Rise and Fall of the Notorious Nazi Leader*, London: Frontline, 2011.

—, *Hess: A Biography*, London: Granada, 1971.

Matzig, Gerhard, "Hitler war für uns ein netter Onkel," *Süddeutche Zeitung*, May 20, 2010.

Mecklenburg, Jens, ed., *Handbuch deutscher Rechtsextremismus*, Berlin: Verlag GmbH, 1996.

Michaeslen, Sven "Niklas Frank," *Süddeutsche Zeitung*, issue 11, 2014.

Millot, Lorraine, "Albert Speer, 63 ans, est architecte. Comme son homonyme de père, le bâtisseur de Hitler. Mais liu a choisi Francfort la libérale. Tel père, quell fils?" *Libération*, February 10, 1998.

Moors, Markus and Moritz Pfeiffer, *Heinrich Himmlers Taschenkalender 1940*, Paderborn: Verlag Ferdinand Schöningh GmbH, 2013.

Morin, Roc, "An Interview With Nazi Leader Hermann Göring's Great-Niece: How do you cope with evil ancestry?" *The Atlantic*, October 16, 2013.

"Nazi Leader's Grandson Fined Over Online Quotes," *Reuters*, January 24, 2002.

Nieden, Suzanne, "Banalitäten aus dem Schlafzimmer derb Macht zu den Tagebuchaufzeichnungen von Margarete Himmler," *Werkstatt Gichichte*, 2000, 94–100.

Nissen, Margret, *Sind Sie die Tochter Speer?*, Cologne: Bastei Lübbe, 2007; München: Deutsche Verlags-Anstalt, 2005.

Noakes, Jeremy and Geoffrey Pridham, *Nazism, 1919–1945. Volume 2: State, Economy, and Society, 1933–1939*, Exeter: University of Exeter Press, 1984.

Norden, Eric, "Albert Speer, Hitler's Architect," *Playboy* 18, no. 6, June 1971.

O'Connor, Gary, *The Butcher of Poland: Hitler's Lawyer Hans Frank*, Staplehurt: Spellmount Publisher's Ltd, 2013.

Oeser, Alexandra, *Enseigner Hitler. Les adolescents allemands face au passé nazi en Allemagne. Appropriations, interprétations et usages de l'histoire*, Paris: Editions de la Maison des sciences de l'homme, 2010.

Paxton, Robert Owen, *Vichy France: Old Guard, and New Order 1940–1944*, preface by S. Hoffman, French trans. C. Bertrand, Paris: Seuil, 1999.

Picker, Henry, *Hitlers Tischgespräche im Führerhauptquartier*, Berlin: Propyläen Verlag, 2003.

Posner, Gerald, *Hitler's Children: Sons and Daughters of Leaders of the Third Reich Talk about Their Fathers and Themselves*, New York: Random House, 1991.

Posner, Gerald L. and John Ware, *Mengele: The Complete Story*, New York: Cooper Square Press, 2000.

Prazan, Michaël, *Einsatzgruppen: Les commandos de la mort Nazis*, Paris: Seuil, 2010.

Raben, Mia, "MS–Vergangenheit: Der lebenslange Schatten," *Der Spiegel*, February 7, 2004.

Raimbault, Marie-Pierre and Michael Grynszpan, *Descendants de nazis. L'héritage infernal*, 2010, France: Bonne Pioche Télévision.

Rees, Laurence, *The Dark Charisma of Adolf Hitler: Leading Millions into the Abyss*, London: Ebury Press, 2012; *Adolf Hitler: La séduction du diable*, French trans. S. Taussig and P. Lucchini, Paris: Albin Michel, 2013.

Rolf Mengele, in an interview with Gerald L. Posner, 1985, transcript.

Rosenberg, Alfred, The Myth of the Twentieth Century, trans. James Whisker, Newport Beach: Noontide Press, 1982.

Schaake, Erich, *Hitler et les femmes: Leur role dabs l'asension du Führer*, Paris: Michel Lafon, 2012.

Schaal, Hans Dieter, *Hans Dieter Schaal, In-between: Exhibition Architecture*, Stuttgart: Edition Axel Menges, 1999.

Schenk, Dieter, *Hans Frank: Hitlers Konjurist und Generalgouverneur*, Frankfurt: Fischer Verlag, 2006.

Schermann, Serge, "Voicing Doubt, Son Gets 2d Autopsy on Hess," *New York Times*, August 22, 1987.

—, "Hess is Buried Secretly by Family; Son is Reported to Suffer Stroke," *New York Times*, August 25, 1987.

Schirach, Henriette von, *Der Preis der Herrlichkeit: erfahrene Zeitgeschichte*, Munich: Herbig, 1981.

Schirmacher, Frank and Hubert Spiegel, "Günter Grass: La tache sur mon passé," *Le Monde*, August 17, 2006.

Schmidt, Matthias, *Albert Speer: La fun d'un mythe*, French trans. J. M. Argelès, Paris: Belfond, 1983.

Schramm, Hilde, *Meine Lehrerin, Dr. Dora Lux 1882–1959*, Reinbek: Rowohlt Verlag, 2012.

Schröm, Oliver and Andrea Röpke, *Stille Hilfe für braune Kameraden: Das geheime Netzwerk der Alt-und Neonazis*, Berlin: Ch. Links Verlag, 2001

Sekkai, Kahina, "Gudrun Himmler, la 'Princesse du Nazisme,'" *Paris Match*, September 6, 2011.

Sereny, Gitta, *Albert Speer: His Battle with Truth*, New York: Vintage, 1996.

—, *Au fond des ténèbres*, Paris: Denoël, 1974, republished in 2007.

Sigmund, Anna Maria, *Les Femmes du III Reich*, trans. J. Bourlois, Paris; Jean-Clause Lattès, 2004; *Women of the Third Reich*, Richmond Hill: NDE Publishing, 2000.

Smoltczyk, Alexander, "2022 World Cup in Qatar: The Desert Dreams of German Architect Albert Speer," *Der Spiegel Online International*, June 1, 2012, http://www.spiegel.de/international/spiegel/german-architect-albert-speer-plans-for-the-2022-world-cup-in-qatar-a-836154.html.

Speer, Albert, *Au coeur du Troisème Reich*, French trans. M. Brottier, Paris: Fayard, 1976; *Inside the Third Reich. Memoirs by Albert Speer*, trans. Richard and Clara Winston, New York: Macmillan, 1970.

—, *Journal de Spandau*, Paris: Robert Laffont, 1976; *Spandau: The Secret Diaries*, trans. Richard and Clara Winston, New York/Toronto: Macmillan, 1976.

Speer, Albert, Jr., *Die intelligente Stadt*, Stuttgart: Deutsche Verlags-Anstalt, 1992.

—, "Frankfurt ist ein Modell für die Welt," *Wirtschaft Frankfurter Allegemeine*, August 25, 2013.

Stringer, Ann, "No One Loves a Policeman," *The Pittsburg Press*, July 13, 1945.

Schwabe, Alexandre, "Interview mit Niklas Frank zur Speer-Debatte: 'Das ewige Herumgeschmuse der Kinder ist lacherlich,'" *Der Spiegel Online*, May 13, 2005, http://www.spiegel.de/politik/deutschland/interview-mit-niklas-frank-zur-speer-debatte-das-ewige-herumgeschmuse-der-kinder-ist-laecherlich-a-355767.html.

Trevor-Roper, Hugh, *The Last Days of Hitler*, Chicago: University of Chicago Press, 1992.

Van der Vat, Dan, *The Good Nazi: The Life and Lies of Albert Speer*, New York: Houghton Mifflin, 1997.

Vincent, Marie-Bénédicte, *La Dénazification*, Paris: Perrin, 2008.

Weber, Anne, *Vaterland*, Paris: Seuil, 2015.

Welzer Harald, *Les Exécuteurs. Des hommes normaux aux meurtriers de masse*, Paris: Gallimard, 2007.

Welzer, Harald, Sabine Möller, and Karoline Tschuggnall, *Opa war kein Nazi: Nationalsozialismus und Holocaust im Familiengedächtnis*, Frankfurt: Fischer Taschenbuch Verlag, 2002.

Westemeier, Jens, *Himmlers Kreiger: Joachim Peiper und die Waffen-SS in Kreig und Nachkriegszeit*, vol. 1, Paderborn: Verlag Ferdinand Schöning GmbH, 2014.

Westernhagen, Dörte von, *Die Kinder der Täter: Das Dritte Reich un die Generation danach*, Munich: Kösel Verlag, 1985.

Ze'evi, Chanoch, *Hitler's Children*, Israel: Film Movement, 2012. DVD.

Zentner, Christian and Friedemann Bedürftig, *Das grosse Lexikon des Dritten Reiches*, Munich: Südwest Verlag, 1985.

ACKNOWLEDGMENTS

All my thanks to:

Jean-François Braunstein, for his advice and corrections.

Stéphan Crasnianski, my brother, for his ideas.

Serge Lentz, for his careful reading and suggestions.

Olivier Manzoni, for his corrections and translations.

Orly Rezlan, for his relevance and patience at every challenge.

Pascal Tutin, for his helpful advice.

Emmanuel Delille and Torsten Lüdtke for their research.

Anna Olekhnovych, for the list of cited works.

I would like to thank my editors Olivier Nora and Juliette Joste at Grasset for their inestimable help in bringing this book to publication.

To my family and friends, for supporting me and reminding me of priorities.